To the Student

Mathematicians need to know how to write. They write the results of their research. They explain math to others. Mathematicians communicate so that what they know can help people improve their lives. Even if you don't become a mathematician, you will be writing about numbers. You may have to write a letter explaining that you can afford a loan or describing how to calculate the cost of doing a project.

The lessons in this book will give you practice writing about math. (See the Writing Checklist on page 75 for general help with writing.) You'll learn skills for school, such as how to take notes and how to answer essay questions. You'll also learn math writing skills that you'll need in your life after school, from explaining a chart to writing a persuasive letter.

Writing in Mathematics is divided into six units that cover math writing and skills. There are also lessons to help you become better at everyday math writing.

Developing Math Skills. In this unit, you'll practice taking notes so that you can remember information you learn from books and from speakers. This unit also deals with ways to solve math problems by thinking as you write and by describing how you have worked a problem.

Real-Life Math. This unit shows you how you use and write about math every day. You will compute a recipe, estimate the costs of running a car, use math to make points in a persuasive letter, and analyze figures from a bar graph.

Writing Math Reports. Writing a report is a great way to think about and understand a math topic. The lessons in this unit break down the steps a writer goes through to create a report. By the time you finish, you will know how to choose a topic, research it, write it, and revise it to create a polished paper.

Thinking of Math in Words. These lessons give you a chance to think about math in a new way—in words. In this unit, you'll invent a logic game, explain the concept of one million, and write a lesson that teaches math to children.

Math at Work. The jobs mentioned in this unit show math at work. You must know math to be successful at almost any job, but you must also be able to explain the process you used to find your numbers. For example, in this unit you'll write an estimate for a carpenter's bid and think about starting your own business. You'll also write about the weather and explain baseball statistics.

Applying Math. Applying your knowledge of math can help you make sense of the world. In this unit, you will use math to decide if you should take a job and to write a speech that explains financial data. You'll also analyze your budget and track your nutrition.

Writing about math can help you understand the world. It is also something you'll use in your daily life. With practice, you can become a better writer. We hope that this book will help you learn this process.

1 Taking Notes
Reading

What You'll LEARN   Taking notes from something you read isn't a skill you'll use only in school. Often, people take notes to help them in their jobs. For example, someone might have to take notes about how to calculate the interest on a loan for college or to start a business.

What You'll DO   Use a chapter of a math book that you are using in your classroom to try this way of taking notes.

What You'll WRITE   Before you begin to take notes, skim what you're reading to find the general outline of the material. To skim, look at the headings and subheadings. Then look at the pictures and graphs. Go back to the beginning and read the introduction. Then read the final paragraphs, which often summarize the chapter. Write your notes here.

1. What is the main topic of the chapter? _____

_____

_____

_____

_____

As you prepare to take notes, keep these tips in mind:

You don't have to write in sentences.

Write important words or phrases.

Write the main points or the central idea of the reading.

Write, step by step, how to solve problems.

2. What information is given in this chapter to help you understand this topic?

_____

_____

_____

_____

_____

3. Select another chapter from the math book. Skim for the main topic of that chapter and supporting explanation. When you have finished, you should have a good idea of what is important in the reading you have just done.

Main idea: _____

_____

First step in solving a problem: _____

_____

_____

_____

Second step: _____

_____

_____

_____

Third step: _____

_____

_____

_____

Use another piece of paper to complete your notes.

4. If you do not understand the material, reread it. Check to see if there are any diagrams that might explain what you don't understand. Review examples step by step. If you still don't understand, ask another student or your teacher for help.

5. When you have finished taking notes, review them. You might want to highlight or underline the most important words in what you wrote. Use your notes to write an explanation of what you just read for another student. _____

_____

_____

_____

_____

_____

_____

_____

_____

2 Taking Notes
Listening

What You'll LEARN

Taking notes while you listen is a skill you will use throughout your life. At some point, you will probably have to listen and then write directions on how to compute the cost of something, for example. This activity will show you how to take good notes while you're listening to someone.

What You'll DO

Keep these tips in mind as you listen to a math lecture:

Much of math is symbols. Make sure you understand them before you write them.

Don't write everything. Write only the key points.

Write in phrases, not sentences.

If the teacher writes on the board, the point is probably important. Copy in your notebook.

What You'll WRITE

Before you begin, review this list of questions. Then fill in the blanks.

1. What is the topic of the lecture or speech? _____

_____

2. What do I already know about the topic? _____

_____

_____

_____

_____

3. What information do I hope to gain? _____

_____

_____

_____

_____

4. What audience does the speaker intend to reach? _____

_____

_____

As you listen to the presentation, keep the following questions in mind. Fill in the answers as you hear them.

5. What is the central point the speaker is making? (You can tell when a speaker is making a central point when he or she uses phrases like "This is the most difficult, and most important, part of the problem.") _____

_____

_____

_____

6. When the teacher demonstrates how to solve a math problem, write the solution step by step. _____

_____

_____

_____

_____

7. Write the steps of another example. _____

_____

_____

_____

_____

8. At the end of a presentation, a speaker usually will restate the important information. How does the speaker summarize his or her lecture? _____

_____

_____

_____

_____

_____

After you have listened to the lecture, review your notes. Rewrite what you can't read. Highlight or underline important points. Work a sample problem or two to make sure you understand the lesson.

LESSON 3 Math Methods
Guess and Test

What You'll LEARN You will learn to use the Guess and Test method of finding the solutions to math problems.

What You'll DO Choose a math problem in your textbook. By the time you have guessed the answer to the problem, you will have another way to think about finding the answer to math problems.

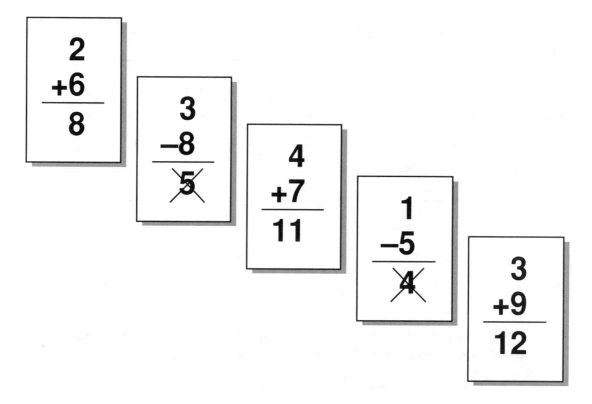

$$\begin{array}{r} 2 \\ +6 \\ \hline 8 \end{array}$$

$$\begin{array}{r} 3 \\ -8 \\ \hline \cancel{5} \end{array}$$

$$\begin{array}{r} 4 \\ +7 \\ \hline 11 \end{array}$$

$$\begin{array}{r} 1 \\ -5 \\ \hline \cancel{4} \end{array}$$

$$\begin{array}{r} 3 \\ +9 \\ \hline 12 \end{array}$$

What You'll WRITE Answer these questions.

1. Look at the problem you've chosen. Based on what you know, make your best guess about the answer. Write a sentence that explains your estimated answer and how you reached it. _____

_____

_____

_____

_____

2. Check your estimate against the numbers in the problem. Does it make sense? Ask yourself, "Can I substitute my guess in a formula?" Write a sentence explaining how you checked your work. _____

_____

_____

_____

_____

3. Use your work in question 2 above to make another guess. Ask yourself, "Should my guess be greater or less than my first guess?" Write how you found this answer. Is it right? If not, write how you will guess and test another answer. _____

_____

_____

_____

_____

_____

_____

_____

_____

_____

_____

4. Look at another problem. Write a paragraph explaining how you used the Guess and Test method to find your answer. _____

_____

_____

_____

_____

_____

_____

LESSON 4 Math Methods
Problem Solving

What You'll LEARN Solving math problems is easier if you have more than one method to use. You'll learn how to use alternate methods to help you understand math.

What You'll DO You'll solve one problem in two ways. Then you'll write a summary of how you used these methods to solve the problem.

What You'll WRITE Find a math problem in your book. Solve the problem. Then answer these questions to help you develop new ways to think about the problem.

1. Write the steps you used to solve the problem. _____

_____

_____

_____

_____

_____

2. Which steps worked well? Which ones gave you trouble? _____

_____

_____

_____

_____

_____

_____

3. What other method could you have used to solve the problem? Write the steps here. Be creative. _____

_____

_____

_____

_____

_____

_____

_____

_____

4. What kinds of problems would be best solved using the first method? Which would be best solved using the second method? Why? _____

_____

_____

_____

_____

_____

_____

_____

_____

_____

_____

LESSON 5 Math Methods
Working Backward

What You'll LEARN
Sometimes, looking at a problem in a new way helps you understand it. In this exercise, you'll work backward to understand a math idea.

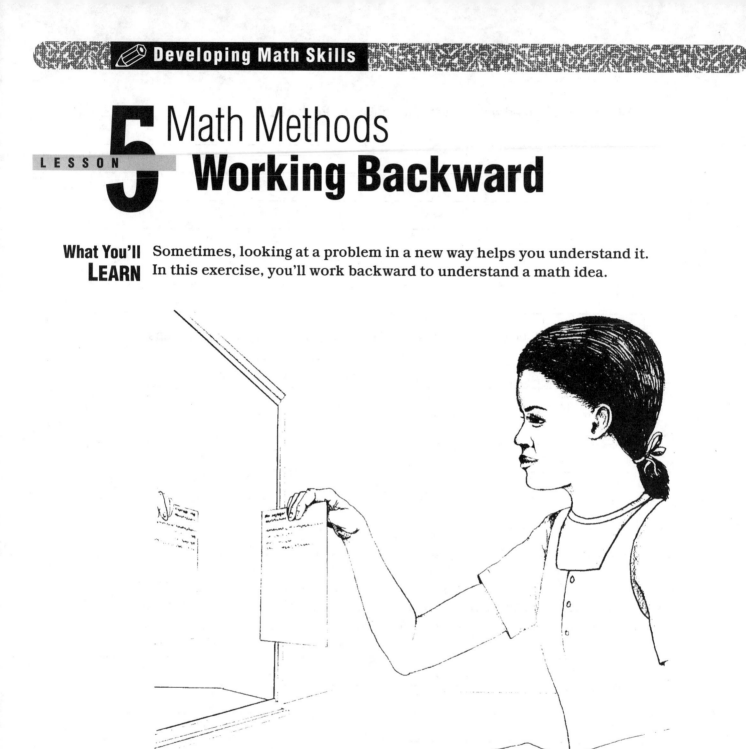

What You'll DO
Ask your teacher for the answer to a math problem in your math book. A word problem is best. Look at the answer and the question. Now think about how you could work backward to understand the question. This technique can come in handy. A painter, for instance, might be given a set amount that a client can spend. The painter would have to work backward to see if he or she could do the job for the money offered.

What You'll WRITE

Answer these questions to work backward to solve a math problem.

1. Write the answer here. _____

_____

_____

_____

2. Write the question here. _____

_____

_____

_____

3. Look at the answer again. How can you work backward to find the question? (For example, imagine that a client has $5,000 to spend. What factors had to be considered to reach that figure?) _____

_____

_____

_____

_____

_____

_____

_____

_____

_____

4. Write another way to reach the same answer to the question. _____

_____

_____

_____

_____

_____

_____

_____

_____

_____

6 Math Methods
LESSON Using Mental Math

What You'll LEARN

Strategies for doing math in your head, without paper and pencil, are important for making everyday life easier. This could help you when you're making change or figuring out how many pairs of jeans you can buy with the amount of money you have.

What You'll DO

Try these methods for quick computing. Then explain in words how each one works.

1. When adding, round to the nearest ten or hundred to eliminate regrouping. Add the rounded numbers; then add or subtract by the amount you rounded. For example:

    $39 + 38 = ?$

    Round 39 up to 40 and add: $40 + 38 = 78$
    Subtract the amount by which you rounded up: $78 - 1 = 77$

    _____

    _____

2. When adding or subtracting, add or subtract by place value. In other words, add or subtract the hundreds, tens, and ones separately. Then add the results to get the answer. For example:

    $467 + 459 = ?$

    a. Add the hundreds: $400 + 400 = 800$
    Add the tens: $60 + 50 = 110$
    Add the ones: $7 + 9 = 16$
    Add the results: $800 + 110 + 16 = 926$

    $899 - 371 = ?$

    _____

    _____

    b. Subtract the hundreds: $800 - 300 = 500$
    Subtract the tens: $90 - 70 = 20$
    Subtract the ones: $9 - 1 = 8$
    Add the results: $500 + 20 + 8 = 528$

    _____

    _____

3. When multiplying, round one number up or down to a factor that is easy to multiply in your head. Usually, these are multiples of 10. Then multiply by the remaining factor, and add or subtract to find the final answer. For example:

$46 \times 13 = ?$

Round 13 down to 10 and multiply: $46 \times 10 = 460$
Multiply: $46 \times 3 = 138$
Add the results: $460 + 138 = 598$

$46 \times 19 = ?$

_____

_____

What You'll WRITE Try the mental math methods above with these problems. Then explain, in complete sentences, how you arrived at your answer.

1. $867 + 32.$ _____

_____

_____

2. $738 - 532.$ _____

_____

_____

3. $39 + 39.$ _____

_____

_____

4. $59 \times 23.$ _____

_____

_____

5. $75 \times 18.$ _____

_____

_____

LESSON 7

Explaining Math
Writing a Lesson

What You'll LEARN Often, the best way to understand something is to explain it so that someone else can understand it.

What You'll DO Choose a math lesson that you find difficult to understand. This is your chance to help someone else—and yourself—understand the concept.

Keep these tips in mind as you organize your lesson:

1. If necessary, include a brief review of what students need to know to understand this concept.

2. Explain unfamiliar terms.

3. Use a step-by step process, explaining each step.

4. Give examples.

5. Explain the lesson in more than one way. If your "student" doesn't understand it when you explain it the first way, try another explanation or another way to solve the problem.

6. Show how the information in the lesson can apply to your "student's" real life.

What You'll WRITE Use this page to write your lesson. If you need more space, use another piece of paper. When you have finished, try it out on a friend to see if he or she understands it. If not, identify the confusing parts and revise them.

8 Explaining Math
LESSON
Writing a Real-Life Test

What You'll LEARN
You'll gain insight into how teachers construct word problems for tests by writing your own.

What You'll DO
Think about the important concepts in a math lesson that you're studying. Then create a test designed to check other students' understanding of these concepts. As you write your questions, think about these points:

1. Teachers often want to see if students understand the main point of what they've been studying.

   You can do that by creating a question that specifically asks for the main point.

2. Most tests contain a wide variety of problems intended to show that students can apply their knowledge to different situations.

   A test about fractions, for example, might have the student answer questions about adjusting a recipe, figuring slices of pie, and comparing the price rise of different stocks.

3. Questions may also ask the student to go beyond the information in the text.

   The student may have to draw conclusions, make inferences (logical guesses), or predict outcomes. By doing this, students prove they can think beyond what's on the page.

4. You have probably noticed that questions on tests tend to proceed in order, from the easiest to the most difficult.

   This can help focus students' thinking and prepare them to handle harder questions.

What You'll WRITE Write math questions on the lines below. Write questions that will show whether students understand and can apply the principles of the lesson. Don't forget to include the answers to the questions.

1. _____

_____

_____

_____

2. _____

_____

_____

_____

3. _____

_____

_____

_____

4. _____

_____

_____

_____

5. _____

_____

_____

_____

6. _____

_____

_____

_____

7. _____

_____

_____

_____

9 Everyday Math

LESSON

Keeping a Math Journal

What You'll LEARN
Keeping a math journal will make you aware of how you use math every day.

What You'll DO
Set aside part of a notebook to take daily notes on how you use math. Examples include buying lunch, estimating costs, and keeping track of your time. Write in your journal every day for two weeks.

Here is an example of a journal entry for one student:

May 12. Today I bought a few groceries for my family. Mom had given me $5 and a list. On the list, she had written: lettuce, tomatoes, bread, and peanut butter. I wanted to buy some ice cream, too, but when I added the prices of all of the things on the list, I didn't have enough money.

What You'll WRITE
Answer these questions for your first entry, using complete sentences. Then write the others in your notebook. At the end of the two weeks, you will write about what you've learned.

1. Describe one way you used math during the day. _____

_____

_____

_____

2. What math skills did you use to do this?_____

_____

_____

_____

3. Describe a way in which you saw someone else use math today. _____

_____

_____

_____

4. What math skills did the person need? _____

_____

_____

5. List any other ways in which you saw math being used or you used it yourself.

_____

_____

Complete the following questions after you have kept your math journal for two weeks.

6. Based on your observations and your use of math, which math skills seem to be the most important in your life now? _____

_____

_____

_____

7. Which math skills do you think you need the most work on, based on your notes for the two weeks? _____

_____

_____

_____

_____

8. How will you develop these skills? _____

_____

_____

_____

_____

10 Analyzing Information
LESSON
Creating a Bar Graph

What You'll LEARN

By sorting and classifying raw information, you can create a bar graph that organizes information visually. A bar graph is often used when people want to compare things. After you have built the graph, you can write a caption for the graph that explains it.

Here is an example of a bar graph. In this case, the information is shown as a series of horizontal bars. Bar graphs can also be constructed so that the bars run vertically. In this bar graph, the bottom line, or axis, lists the average miles per gallon. The vertical axis lists types of vehicles.

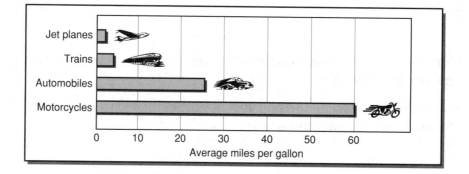

When you look at this bar graph, it is easy to compare the gas mileage for each of these vehicles.

What You'll Do

You are a newspaper reporter writing a story about the costs of foods at different professional sporting events in your city. Below is the information you gathered.

HOCKEY
hot dog: $2.50
soft drink: $3.00
nachos: $4.00
candy bar: $2.50

BASEBALL
hot dog: $3.00
soft drink: $2.50
nachos: $4.00
candy bar: $3.00

FOOTBALL
hot dog: $3.50
soft drink: $4.00
nachos: $4.50
candy bar: $3.00

1. Use this space to create a bar graph that displays the information about the costs of foods at different sporting events.

1. What did you learn about the costs of foods at the different sporting events?

_____

_____

_____

_____

2. You will use your bar graph to illustrate a front-page story called "Are You Getting Your Money's Worth?" You know that readers will probably read the headline first. Then they will look at the graph. Finally, they will look at the caption under the graph. Write the caption for the graph, using what you learned from your research.

Caption: _____

_____

_____

_____

_____

_____

11 Gathering Data
A Public-Attitude Survey

LESSON

What You'll LEARN

Companies design surveys to learn what the public thinks about an issue. In this activity, you will learn how to design a public-attitude survey and then analyze the answers you get.

What You'll DO

Designing a public-attitude survey involves writing questions that help you gather information, or data, that you can analyze. One example is whether nuclear energy is good or bad. Choose an issue that people disagree about. Then design a public-attitude survey that will show where people stand on the issue.

Here are some guidelines to use in designing your survey:

1. Narrow your topic. If it is too broad, you will get answers that are too broad in return. For example, if you ask questions about whether people do or do not like pollution, you will get predictable answers that do not help you understand a specific situation.

2. Avoid bias. Bias, or prejudice, can make your survey inaccurate. Write your questions so that they are neutral and do not show how you feel about the topic. For example, if you ask "Don't you think nuclear energy is a bad thing?" the answers you get might not reflect how people really feel.

3. Narrow your questions. In most cases, giving people questions that are too open-ended will not allow you to compare opinions. An example of an open-ended question is: "How do you feel about pollution?" Instead, ask yes or no questions. Then you will be able to count the answers more easily.

Here is one survey a student wrote to help her find out what people would do to reduce air pollution:

PUBLIC OPINION SURVEY

Hello, my name is ——————— . I am a student at ——————— school. My class is gathering information about the issue of ——————— . Would you share with me how you feel about it?

If "No," say thank you. If "Yes," continue.

1. In your opinion, is air pollution a health problem in our city?

               YES   NO   UNDECIDED

2. Would you be willing to use your car less in order to reduce air pollution?

               YES   NO   UNDECIDED

3. Would you be willing to stop using your backyard barbecue in order to reduce air pollution?

               YES   NO   UNDECIDED

What You'll WRITE Use this page to develop your survey.

1. What topic do you want to gather information about? _____

_____

2. What questions could you ask to find out public opinion on this issue?

a. _____

_____

b. _____

_____

c. _____

_____

d. _____

_____

Use this checklist to think about the survey you designed:

☐ Are the questions you wrote free of bias?

☐ Are the questions easy for people to understand?

☐ Will you find out what you want from these questions?

Now take your survey. Keep these points in mind:

Decide who your audience is, and ask people in that group.

Decide whether to take your survey by mail, by phone, or in person.

Ask enough people so that your results are a good sample of the way people in your audience feel.

3. On a separate piece of paper, analyze your results. Figure the percentage of people who answered your questions in each way.

4. Create a graph in the space below to help you understand the information. See Lesson 10, Analyzing Information: Creating a Bar Graph, on page 20, if you need information on creating a bar graph.

12 Using Math
LESSON 12

Writing a Persuasive Letter

What You'll LEARN

Some people think that only words can persuade people to change their minds. However, you can use math to make a very convincing argument.

What You'll Do

Imagine that the school board has just said that no students will be allowed to wear shorts in school. (You may also choose another issue that is relevant to your school.) You want to fight this new ruling. Take a survey among students to learn their opinions. Then write a persuasive letter to the school board explaining why you think that its position is wrong.

To write a persuasive letter, keep these hints in mind:

In a persuasive letter, you are trying to convince someone that your opinion is right.

Most persuasive letters begin with a statement that gives an opinion.

To convince the reader that your opinion is right, you need to include supporting evidence.

Evidence can be facts or, in this case, the opinions of a group of people.

In this case, you will support your opinion with the results from a survey you take among students. See Lesson 11, Gathering Data: A Public-Attitude Survey, on page 22, for information about how to do this.

When you write a letter, you should use this form:

248 Cherry Drive
Northville, CA 95828
January 31, 1996

Dr. Norman Cleary
Northville Public School District
Northville, CA 95828

Dear Dr. Cleary:

Sincerely,
Dorothy Stanford

Dorothy Stanford

What You'll WRITE Use this page to write your letter. Remember to make your argument clearly. Use the results of your survey to support what you say. Check your grammar and spelling.

_____

_____

_____

_____

_____

_____

_____

_____

_____

_____

_____

_____

_____

_____

_____

_____

_____

_____

_____

_____

_____

_____

_____

_____

_____

_____

_____

13 Using Fractions
LESSON
Computing a Recipe

What You'll LEARN
Anyone who cooks knows that recipes sometimes have to be changed. You may want to serve more or less of the food than the recipe yields. This activity will give you practice in this skill.

What You'll DO
Your class is having an International Day. Everyone is bringing a dish from a different part of the world. Your recipe, though, has to be changed so that it can feed your class.

What You'll WRITE
Choose a recipe from another part of the world. Then answer these questions in complete sentences.

1. How many people does the recipe serve now? _____

_____

2. How would you change the amount of the recipe's ingredients
to serve your class? _____

_____

_____

_____

3. How would you change the cooking directions to cook that many portions? (You may have to make the recipe in batches.) _____

_____

_____

_____

_____

_____

4. Rewrite your recipe so that it will serve your class. Be sure to change the instructions for cooking if necessary. _____

_____

_____

_____

_____

_____

_____

_____

_____

_____

_____

_____

_____

_____

_____

_____

_____

LESSON 14 Estimating The Costs of Running a Car

What You'll LEARN

Knowing the cost of running a car is important. Figuring the car's gas mileage will help you plan when you will need to buy gas and how much money you will need to spend to reach some destination. By knowing how much your car costs to operate, you can make sure you save enough to pay for those costs.

What You'll DO

Imagine that you are going to sell your family's car. The only catch is that the person who wants to buy it is concerned that the costs of running the car are too high. Your job is to find out those costs. You will be figuring the miles per gallon your car gets. You will also find out the costs for repairs and maintenance.

What You'll WRITE

Complete the following activities using complete sentences. Then write a letter to the buyer explaining the costs of running your car.

1. Find out how many miles your family's car will run on a gallon of gasoline. To do this, follow this procedure:

   a. Note the odometer reading when the tank is full. The odometer is the instrument on the dashboard that measures the distance that a car travels.

   _____

   b. When you need gas again, fill the car up completely, and write the number of gallons that you received.

   _____

c. Subtract the first odometer reading from the current reading. This is the number of miles you have driven on a tank of gas.

_____

d. Divide the number of miles by the number of gallons of gas you used. The answer is the number of miles per gallon (MPG).

_____

e. Write your MPG and how you reached it here. Also write the costs of gas for a mile.

_____

2. Find the records of what your family spends on the car during a year, or have the person who pays the bills tell you the costs. List repairs, tires, and oil changes, as well as smaller items like window-washing fluid. Write the yearly cost for the car here in complete sentences. _____

_____

_____

_____

_____

3. Write a letter to the person who wants to buy the car. Explain the miles per gallon that your car gets and the maintenance and repair costs for a year. _____

_____

_____

_____

_____

_____

_____

_____

_____

_____

_____

_____

_____

_____

15 Writing a Short Paper
LESSON

Explaining Math History

What You'll LEARN
Being able to explain the history of math can help you understand its use in other cultures and how we use it today.

What You'll DO
Choose a way that people do math in other cultures today or a historical method of doing math. Examples include the Chinese abacus, the Mayan invention of zero, or the Babylonian numbering system.

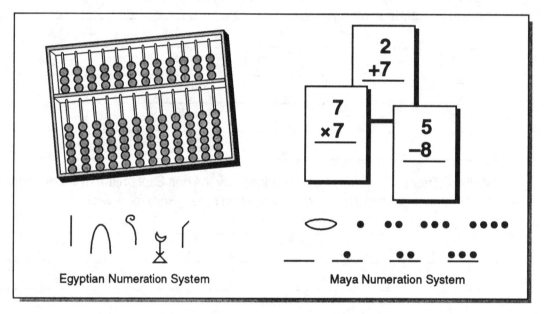

Egyptian Numeration System   Maya Numeration System

What You'll WRITE
Research the history of mathematics, and find a system or discovery that interests you. Answer these questions. On the next page write a short report about what you learned.

1. What is the system or discovery? _____

_____

_____

_____

2. How does it work? Explain it. _____

_____

_____

_____

_____

3. Who are the people involved? _____

_____

_____

4. When was this system invented or used? _____

_____

_____

5. Where was this system used? _____

_____

_____

6. Write a report below that tells the history of the system or discovery, explains it, and describes how it was, or is, used. Remember to begin each paragraph with a topic sentence that explains the point of the paragraph. Then include supporting evidence for your topic sentence. Use another piece of paper if necessary.

_____

_____

_____

_____

_____

_____

_____

_____

_____

_____

_____

_____

_____

_____

_____

_____

_____

_____

_____

_____

16 Writing a Report

LESSON

Choosing a Topic

What You'll LEARN

You will learn how to decide on a topic for a math report that is broad enough to be interesting but narrow enough to be done well. Reports about math can be about people who have been important in math, such as Pythagoras. They can also be about the history of an idea in math, such as the invention of the computer.

What You'll DO

Read how one student decided on a report topic.

1. She knew that she was interested in writing about the history of the calendar.

2. She researched the topic. She found out that whole books had been written about the history of calendars, so the topic was too broad.

3. She thought about what she was interested in about the subject and settled on these ideas: the calendar of the ancient Babylonians, the modern calendar, and the Mayan calendar.

4. She went to the library. She learned that there was too much information about the modern calendar and too little about the calendar of the ancient Babylonians. She chose the topic "The Ancient Mayan Calendar" for her report.

What You'll WRITE

Answer these questions to help you decide on a topic.

1. What general topics am I interested in?

   a. _____

   b. _____

   c. _____

   d. _____

2. Which topic am I most interested in? Why? _____

   _____

   _____

   _____

   _____

   _____

3. How can I narrow this topic so that I will be able to write a research paper about it? (Go to the library to find out what information there is about your topic in books and magazines.)

a. _____

b. _____

c. _____

4. Choose the narrow topic that most interests you: _____

---

5. Begin your research by listing books and magazine articles that you will use as sources for your report. These sources are called the *bibliography.* If you will be using the *Readers' Guide to Periodical Literature,* follow these steps:

a. The *Guides* are listed by year. Check the years in which you think your subject may be mentioned.

b. Subjects are listed alphabetically. If there are no entries, try a related subject.

c. If the listing for your subject says *See* _____, look under the other term. If there are subheadings, look under the one that is closest to your topic.

d. Here is a typical entry with its parts explained:

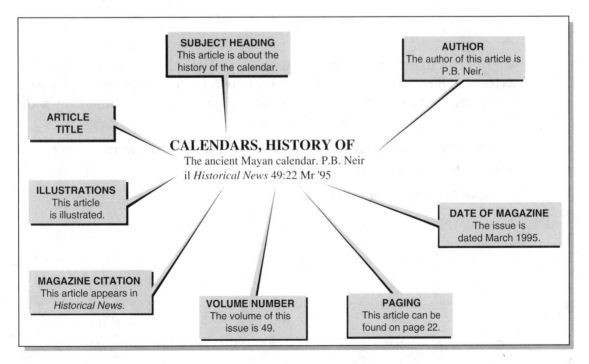

SUBJECT HEADING
This article is about the history of the calendar.

AUTHOR
The author of this article is P.B. Neir.

ARTICLE TITLE

CALENDARS, HISTORY OF
The ancient Mayan calendar. P.B. Neir
il *Historical News* 49:22 Mr '95

ILLUSTRATIONS
This article is illustrated.

DATE OF MAGAZINE
The issue is dated March 1995.

MAGAZINE CITATION
This article appears in *Historical News.*

VOLUME NUMBER
The volume of this issue is 49.

PAGING
This article can be found on page 22.

6. What are the three best sources for the information you want to include in your report? On another piece of paper, list each article, its author, the magazine and date, and the pages the information is on. For each book, list the title, author, publisher, and city and year in which it was published.

17 Writing a Report
LESSON
Taking Notes

What You'll LEARN It's important to keep track of the information you're learning for your report. You'll also learn how to take notes you can later use to write your report.

What You'll DO The easiest way to write a report about a math subject is to begin by organizing the information that you are learning. Taking good notes is important. If you don't, researching and writing a report can seem overwhelming.

What You'll WRITE By answering the questions in this activity, you will have outlined the information from your first article or book. You can then use this information to help you write your report.

1. What questions do you want to answer in your report? _____

_____

_____

_____

You can use a notebook to write information for your report. Some writers find that taking notes on 3-inch by 5-inch cards is helpful. By doing this, they are able to put the cards in the order in which they want to use them when they write their report.

Writers who use this method often write a heading on the card to help them sort the cards later.

Here is one student's example:

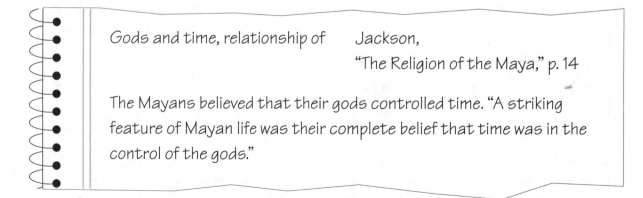

Gods and time, relationship of   Jackson,
"The Religion of the Maya," p. 14

The Mayans believed that their gods controlled time. "A striking feature of Mayan life was their complete belief that time was in the control of the gods."

2. Skim the article or book. All of it may have to do with your topic, but you may only be interested in some of the information available. When you have found what you need, write the name of the book or article, the pages that were helpful, and a summary of what you have learned that will help you answer your question.

_____

_____

_____

_____

_____

_____

_____

_____

_____

_____

3. What evidence or examples does the author give to support his or her arguments or points? _____

_____

_____

_____

_____

_____

_____

_____

_____

4. If an author writes an opinion that you want to include in your report, write it here exactly. Put quotations around the author's words. Also write the page on which the quotation appeared, and who said it if it was someone other than the author.

_____

_____

_____

_____

_____

_____

18 Writing a Report

LESSON

Creating an Outline

What You'll LEARN

Looking at all the notes you've made can be discouraging. How can you organize them so that they make sense? You can create an outline. You can then use your outline to help you write a first draft.

What You'll DO

The first step is to read all the information that you have collected. After that, sort the information into piles with similar main ideas. By then, you'll have the rough organization for your report.

What You'll WRITE

The activities below will help you get your outline started.

1. Look at one of the piles. Write a sentence that describes its general topic.

_____

_____

2. Do the same thing for all of the piles you made. On another piece of paper, write a topic sentence that describes each pile.

Now sort each pile into smaller groups by idea. For example, if the student's pile contained notes about the relationship between the gods and the Mayan calendar, her smaller groups might be:

A. What the gods were
B. How the gods were supposed to control time

3. Write the ideas that you find in one of your piles here. Then use another piece of paper to make a list of ideas for each pile. _____

_____

_____

_____

_____

4. Now you can create an outline. At the top, write the statement that describes your report's topic. Next, put the groups in order in a way that supports the topic. Write a main point for each of these groups. Under these, write phrases that support each main point.

Here is the student's outline:

Statement: The Mayan civilization (1500 B.C. to 900 A.D.) created an accurate calendar. It was the most accurate calendar in the world until the Gregorian calendar was invented in 1582. Although the Mayan civilization largely died out, its calendar shows us its sophistication.

I. Introduction
II. How the Maya developed their calendar
    A. Background about Mayan culture
    B. Relationship between the Mayan calendar and religion

III. How the Mayan calendar worked
    A. How the calendar divided time
    B. How it differs from other calendars

IV. How the Mayan calendar worked
    A. Mayan civilization died out
    B. Other calendars were tried, but none as accurate until Gregorian

IV. Conclusion

4. Use this space to write your own outline, or use another piece of paper.

Statement: _____

I. Introduction: _____

II. _____

    A. _____

    B. _____

III. _____

    A. _____

    B. _____

IV. Conclusion: _____

_____

LESSON 19 Writing a Report
The First Draft

What You'll LEARN
Now that you have your topic narrowed and your research organized, you will learn how to use this information to write a draft of your report.

What You'll DO
Use the information you have gathered and organized to write the first draft of your math report.

What You'll WRITE
Answer the questions on these pages to help you write your first draft.

The introduction. In a report, this is the first paragraph. In the introduction, include sentences that give a brief outline of what you will say in the report.

Here is the student's introduction:

> Among the inventions of the Mayan people was a remarkable calendar. It was complex, but it was also the most accurate calendar in the world for many centuries. The Mayans invented their calendar long before the birth of Christ. It was not until the 1500s that another calendar as accurate was created. The Mayan calendar was an important achievement.

1. Use this space to write an introduction to your report. _____

_____

_____

_____

_____

_____

_____

_____

_____

The body. For the main part of your report, or the body, it is useful to have your outline and notecards at hand. As you begin to write, follow your outline. Use the notes you made to help you write.

One important point to remember is not to plagiarize, or copy exactly, someone's words or ideas. It is fine to use facts that are generally known without crediting a source, but if you use someone's exact words, quote the person. If you use someone's idea or theory, write whose idea or theory it is.

As you make each point on your outline, make sure to include a topic sentence that explains your argument. The student used the following topic sentence in the body of her report:

> The Mayan calendar was set by a complicated system based on the sun.

2. Write the topic sentence for the first point you will make. _____

_____

_____

_____

_____

Follow your topic sentence with evidence from your notes to back it up. For example, the sentence above might be followed with information about what experts think was the importance of the sun in the calendar.

Conclusion. After you have made all the points you want to make in the body of your report, write the concluding paragraph. In this paragraph, you summarize what you have shown in the paper.

Here is the student's conclusion to the report about the Mayan calendar:

> The Mayan civilization did not survive, but it left behind remarkable achievements. One of these was the Mayan calendar. This calendar was based on the sun and the Mayan religion. It was much more complicated than the calendar we use today. It was also the most accurate calendar the world had seen. It was the most accurate calendar in the world for hundreds of years, until the Gregorian calendar was created in 1582.

3. Write your conclusion on another piece of paper.

20 LESSON Writing a Report
Revising and Footnotes

What You'll LEARN

Revising your work and writing the footnotes and bibliography are the final steps in creating your report.

What You'll DO

By *revising* the draft, you have the chance to polish your work. Use this checklist to make your report stronger:

☐ Does your draft match your outline?

☐ Is your writing organized? Does one point lead to the next?

☐ Have you chosen the right words to say exactly what you mean?

☐ Have you checked your grammar?

☐ Have you proofread the report for spelling, capitalization, and punctuation?

Footnotes give credit to the writers whose ideas you are using in your report. They also give readers the ability to learn more about your topic or to check your sources. Use footnotes when you:

quote an author exactly;
use a writer's ideas;
use numbers or statistics.

Footnotes can either be listed at the bottom of the page on which the reference appears or at the end of your report. If they are listed at the end of your report, they are called *endnotes.* They are usually numbered in order throughout the report. Here are the forms for different kinds of footnote sources:

A book:
[1] Jane Jackson, Maya (New York: Shanan Press, 1996), p. 39

A magazine article:
[2] Peter B. Neir, "The Ancient Mayan Calendar," Historical News, March 1995, p. 22

A newspaper article:
[3] "Archaeologists Find Calendar Evidence," by Kelcy Argo, Bedford Chronicle, July 17, 1993

An article from an encyclopedia:
[4] "Maya," Microsoft Encarta Encyclopedia, 1994 ed., p. 917

If you use the same source more than once, you don't have to write all the information again. Instead, you write:

[5] Neir, p. 25

The *bibliography* belongs at the end of your report. In the bibliography, you list the sources you used for your report in alphabetic order. Here is a sample bibliography entry:

Neir, Peter B. "The Ancient Mayan Calendar," <u>Historical News</u>,
    March 1995, p. 22

What You'll WRITE

You'll write a final draft of your report and prepare your footnotes and bibliography.

1. Review the draft and revise it. Use the checklist on page 40 as a guide.

2. Write the first footnote for your report. _____

_____

_____

_____

3. Write your bibliography here. _____

_____

_____

_____

_____

_____

_____

_____

_____

4. Make a final copy of your report.

21 Math Fun
Writing a Logic Game

What You'll LEARN

Completing a logic game can help you make mathematical inferences and use logic. Writing your own logic game will give you a chance to see the process from the point of view of the game's creator.

What You'll DO

First, complete this logic game:

Three families live on the same street.

From these clues, find out which family lives in which house and which family has which hobby.

Write notes on the picture below to help you solve the game.

1. The Joneses live next to the Ramons.

2. The photography lovers do not live next to the family that loves to camp.

3. There are no children in the middle house.

4. The middle family frequently hikes.

5. Jamaica Jones and Sally Barnes go to the same middle school.

6. The family on the right does not take pictures.

7. Sally loves camping with her family.

What You'll WRITE Answer these questions.

1. Write the answer to this logic game. Which family lives in which house? Which family has which hobby? Use complete sentences. _____

_____

_____

_____

_____

2. Now create your own logic game. Make sure it can be answered with the clues you gave. Then give the game to a friend to answer. _____

_____

_____

_____

_____

_____

_____

_____

_____

_____

_____

_____

_____

_____

_____

_____

_____

_____

_____

_____

_____

22 Describing Math
LESSON
What's a Million

What You'll LEARN

Sometimes it is hard to explain large numbers. Even so, understanding how much a million or a billion is can be important. To understand the federal budget, for instance, you have to have an idea of what a million really is.

What You'll DO

Think about what a million is. Write it down in numerals. Now think of ways to explain how much a million is so that someone can understand it.

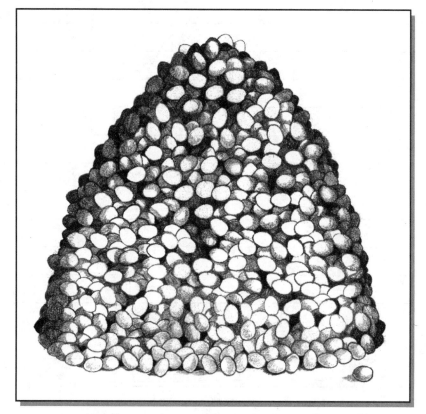

What You'll WRITE Think of three different ways to explain the idea of a million. Your three ways must be descriptive. For example, measure the height of a telephone book laid on its side, and calculate how high a million books would reach or how far they would stretch on the ground.

1. _____

_____

_____

_____

_____

2. _____

_____

_____

_____

_____

3. _____

_____

_____

_____

_____

4. Here's a real challenge. Describe a billion. _____

_____

_____

_____

_____

_____

_____

_____

_____

23 Explaining Math

LESSON

Writing a Book for Children

What You'll LEARN

One of the important skills in math is being able to explain what you know. On these pages, you'll explain a math idea so that third-graders can understand it.

What You'll DO

First, choose a math topic to explain. It could be anything from long division to how to add and subtract fractions.

Look at some math books written for young children. Take notes about methods of teaching that seem clear to you. Then organize what you learned into a written lesson that a third-grader can understand. Write possible ways to illustrate each page.

What You'll WRITE

1. On the rest of this page, outline the steps you will use to teach your lesson.

_____

_____

_____

_____

_____

_____

_____

_____

_____

_____

_____

_____

_____

_____

2. Make a thumbnail sketch (a small version of the pages in your lesson) on this page. Write the words as they would appear. Also write what illustrations or drawings you would like to see. If you need more pages, use another piece of paper.

After you've finished your thumbnail sketch, make a full-sized lesson. Give it to a third-grader to see if he or she understands what you wrote.

24 Estimating

LESSON

Writing a Carpenter's Bid

What You'll LEARN

Before a carpenter is given a contract for new business, he or she must estimate how much the job will cost to do and write a bid letter detailing how much the client will be charged.

What You'll DO

Look at this drawing of a counter for a garage. A homeowner wants you to estimate the cost of materials and labor before he decides if you will build his counter. He wants the counter to be made with plywood and have a plastic surface. Here is the drawing he gave you:

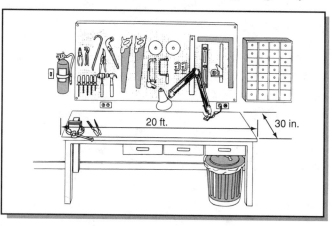

20 ft.   30 in.

Here are the costs you need to figure:

3/4-inch plywood	16 sheets	$6.39 sheet
counter surface	2 rolls	$20.39 roll
nails, contact cement, other supplies		$67.00
labor	30 hours	$20 hour
overhead charge	15% of total	

1. Use this space to figure the costs of the job.

plywood   _____

counter surface   _____

other materials   _____

labor   _____

overhead   _____

What You'll WRITE Use this page to write a bid letter to the homeowner. Follow these rules for writing a business letter. You can refer to Lesson 12, Using Math: Writing a Persuasive Letter, on page 24, for an example of a formal letter.

- ☐ Put your address at the top.

- ☐ Follow that with the date.

- ☐ Leave a line, and write the address of the person you are writing to.

- ☐ Address your letter, "Dear Mr. Baker:".

- ☐ In the body of your letter, first say why you are writing. In this case, you are writing to give Mr. Baker a bid.

- ☐ Explain how you reached your bid.

- ☐ Tell Mr. Baker how long the job will take and when you can start. Also let him know that you want his business.

- ☐ Close with "Sincerely," or "Yours truly." Then sign your name.

2. Write your letter here. _____

_____

_____

_____

_____

_____

_____

_____

_____

_____

_____

_____

_____

_____

_____

_____

_____

_____

_____

_____

25 Planning Costs

LESSON

Working as a Travel Agent

What You'll LEARN

Travel agents have to use math to plan trips for their clients. In this exercise, you'll learn how to calculate vacation costs.

What You'll DO

The Sherr family wants to vacation for one week in a warm, sunny climate during spring break. The family has $4,000 to spend for two adults and two children, aged 5 and 1. Some of the possibilities are described below. Plan three possible vacations for the Sherrs that lie within their budget. You might want to look at Lesson 5, Math Methods: Working Backward.

Arizona resorts:
$450 airfare for adults and children; children under 2 are free.
Mt. Jackson, with pool, tennis, golf: $300 per night; count $40 per day
    for meals for adults, $25 for children
Polmon Resort: includes all meals, pool, horseback riding: $125 per person,
    per night, children 5 and under half price

Caribbean cruises:
Airfare, all meals, and activities are included.
Starlight Lines: two lower-deck connecting cabins, $1600 each adult.
    Upper-deck family cabin, with bigger windows and more space,
    $1800 each adult. Children under 12 half price, 5 and under free.
Triumph Cruises: Family cabin on upper deck, but smaller and older than
    the Starlight Lines ships: $1500 each adult, children under 12 are free
    if they sleep in their parents' cabin

Mexico:
Airfare and hotel packages
Mazatlán: airfare-and-hotel package: $656 per person,
    kids 5 and under free, under 12 half price.
    Meals: $30 per person per day, $15 for children
    No pool; hotel is on beach

Cabo San Lucas:
Airfare-and-hotel package: $875 per person, children 5 and under free, under 12 half price.
    Breakfast and dinner, pool, tennis, and horseback riding included
    Lunches: $7 per person, children half price

What You'll WRITE Write a business letter to the Sherr family explaining what vacations they can afford in each category. See the tips for writing a business letter in the previous activity. In your letter, you can make a recommendation for which vacation you think offers the best deal for the money the Sherr family has to spend.

26 Estimating Costs and Profits
LESSON
Planning a Service Business

What You'll LEARN

You'll learn how to figure the costs and profits of a service business.

What You'll DO

Almost everyone has thought of starting his or her own business. The possibilities are endless, from a lawn-cutting service to a car-detailing business to a baby-sitting cooperative. In this exercise, you'll think about how you could start a business of your own.

What You'll WRITE

Answer these questions in complete sentences. By the end of the activity, you should know whether you can make any money in your business.

1. First, research the market. Is anyone else doing what you want to do? If so, is there enough business in your area for you to succeed, too?

_____

_____

_____

_____

2. What is the competition charging for its product or service? _____

_____

_____

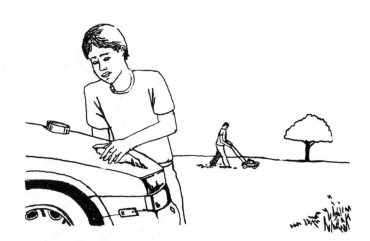

3. Think about what your costs will be. Include the costs of renting space and/or equipment, the costs of materials, the costs of employees if you need any, and the costs of outside services such as printing. Write what your expenses will be.

_____

_____

_____

_____

_____

_____

4. What will you charge for your product or service? How much do you expect to sell? How do your charges compare to what others are charging? _____

_____

_____

_____

_____

_____

5. Write an analysis of the business you want to run. Will it make money? How much? What are your projected sales for the next year? For the next five years?

_____

_____

_____

_____

_____

_____

_____

_____

_____

_____

_____

27 Figuring Discount
LESSON
Writing an Ad for Your Business

What You'll LEARN

You can attract customers to your business by advertising discounts on your service.

What You'll Do

You've started your service business (in Lesson 26), but you'd like more customers. You'd also like to sign up customers for long-term contracts. You've decided to advertise to reach more potential customers.

You've chosen to advertise in a local newspaper. To introduce your business to people, you've decided to offer an introductory special of 50 percent off your service for first-time users.

You've also decided to give discounts to people who sign up to use your service weekly, monthly, and for a year. Figure out what kind of discount you want to offer to attract these long-term customers.

Place Your Ad Here Call Us!!!!!!!!!!!!

Pretty Puppy
WE DO PUPPIES & KITTENS TOO!
HANDLED WITH CARE
289-4405

KIDDIE MINDER
447-6870

EMERALD MAGIC
PLANT-WATERING SERVICES
POOL AREAS, PATIOS AND MUCH MORE
467-3811

MARK'S AUTO CLEANING SERVICE, INC.
• Complete Auto Cleaning
• Vaccuming
• Waxing
737-3070
411 Central Islip Blvd., Lake Ronk

NATURESCAPE
LANDSCAPE MANAGEMENT
• Railrod Ties & Design
• Irrigation Systems
• Sod & Seed Lawns Installed
Commercial & Residential
Weekly Lawn Maintenance Available
FREE ESTIMATES
862-5296
ST. JAMES OFFICE

WRITING IN MATHEMATICS

TEACHER'S RESOURCE MANUAL

WELD COUNTY SCHOOL DISTRICT RE-3 (J)

WELD COUNTY SCHOOL DISTRICT RE-3 (J)

GLOBE FEARON

CONTENTS: Writing in Mathematics

Writing Self-Assessment

Writing Mechanics Checklist

The Writing Process: Brainstorming

The Writing Process: Organizing Ideas

The Writing Process: Drafting a Paragraph

The Writing Process: Checking Your Outline

The Writing Process: Revising

Creating a Bar Graph

Creating a Circle Graph

Writing Word Problems

Creating a Flow Chart to Run a Business

Executive Editor: Barbara Levadi
Project Editors: Lynn W. Kloss, Laura Baselice, and Bernice Golden
Writer: Sandra Widener
Production Manager: Penny Gibson
Production Editor: Nicole Cypher
Marketing Managers: Sandra Hutchison and Nancy Surridge
Interior Electronic Design: Richard Puder Design
Electronic Page Production: Mimi Raihl
Cover Design: Mimi Raihl

Printed in the United States of America.   6 7 8 9 10 04 03 02 01

ISBN: 0835-91896-3

GLOBE FEARON EDUCATIONAL PUBLISHER
Upper Saddle River, New Jersey
www.globefearon.com

To the Teacher

Writing in Mathematics has been created to give your students wide experience in writing about math. The lessons are designed to be used by individual students with little teacher intervention.

The kinds of writing that are covered in this book include responsive math writing, such as journal writing, which improves students' ability to make observations and connections between math and their lives. There are also exercises designed to teach such study skills as taking notes and taking essay tests. The book deals with a wide variety of the critical-thinking skills needed in math. For example, there are lessons that teach how to gather data and how to analyze information. A set of lessons teaches the skills necessary to write a research paper about the history or applications of math. Finally, there are lessons that stress math writing in everyday life and in careers.

Some of the lessons may be best suited to particular kinds of math study. The exercise in which students write about baseball statistics, for example, might be a good accompaniment to a unit on statistics. Many of the other lessons are designed to accompany any topic of math study. For example, the lesson on taking notes instructs students to take notes on a concept in a math book they are using.

This Teacher's Manual contains general suggestions for using these lessons in the classroom. In addition, there are **Teaching Notes** that offer specific suggestions for each lesson. **Extension Activities** provide ways to expand the lessons if students are interested. **Cooperative Learning** offers suggestions for turning these lessons into group projects. **ESL/LEP Strategies** provide ways for teachers to aid students who are learning English as a Second Language and students with Limited English Proficiency.

An **Assessment** section on pages 6-7 offers suggestions for evaluating student writing, and there are reproducible masters (on pages 19 and 20) for students to use for self-assessment. Those and the other reproducible masters in the back of the book can be used to reinforce skills or give students more practice at the writing and thinking skills that math requires. These reproducibles are not lesson specific; they can be adapted for use with many lessons in this book and in mathematics classwork.

This program was planned to provide your students with interesting, varied, and independent exercises that will provide practice in the writing skills needed in math. We hope you find it useful in your classroom.

Correlation to Key Skills in Mathematics

LESSON	MATH SKILLS	WRITING SKILLS	STUDY AND RESEARCH SKILLS	CRITICAL-THINKING SKILLS
1. Taking Notes: Reading		Writing notes	Taking notes	Identifying main ideas
2. Taking Notes: Listening		Writing notes	Taking notes	Identifying main ideas
3. Math Methods: Guess and Test	Problem solving	Writing an explanation		Problem solving
4. Math Methods: Problem Solving	Problem solving	Writing an explanation		Problem solving
5. Math Methods: Working Backward	Problem solving	Writing an explanation		Problem solving
6. Math Methods: Using Mental Math	Mental math	Writing an explanation		
7. Explaining Math: Writing a Lesson		Writing a presentation		Organizing information
8. Explaining Math: Writing a Real-Life Test		Writing essay/story problems	Essay/story problems	Analyzing information
9. Everyday Math: Keeping a Math Journal		Writing a description, writing an analysis		Applying knowledge
10. Analyzing Information: Creating a Bar Graph	Creating a bar graph	Writing an analysis		Analyzing information
11. Gathering Data: A Public-Opinion Survey	Percentages	Writing survey questions		Gathering information
12. Using Math: Writing a Persuasive Letter	Percentages	Writing a persuasive letter		Gathering information
13. Using Fractions: Computing a Recipe	Fractions	Writing an explanantion		
14 Estimating: The Costs of Running a Car	Estimating	Writing an explanation		
15. Writing a Short Paper: Explaining Math History		Writing a short report	Using library materials	Gathering information
16. Writing a Report: Choosing a Topic		Prewriting	Using library materials	
17. Writing a Report: Taking Notes		Writing notes	Taking notes	
18. Writing a Report: Creating an Outline		Creating an outline	Creating an outline	Organizing information

19. Writing a Report: The First Draft		Writing a first draft	Writing a report	Organizing information
20. Writing a Report: Revising and Footnotes		Revising	Using library materials	Organizing information
21. Math Fun: Writing a Logic Game	Logic	Writing a game		Analyzing information
22. Describing Math: What's a Million?	Understanding large numbers	Writing a description		
23. Explaining Math: Writing a Book for Children		Writing a description		Analyzing informaiton
24. Estimating: Writing a Carpenter's Bid	Estimating	Writing an explanation		
25. Planning Costs: Working as a Travel Agent	Making calculations	Writing an explanation		Analyzing information
26. Estimating Costs and Profits: Planning a Service Business	Estimating	Writing an analysis		Analyzing information
27. Figuring Discount: Writing an Ad for Your Business	Percentages	Writing an ad		
28. Using Statistics: Working as a Baseball Writer	Statistics	Writing an explanation		Evaluating information
29. Making Predictions: Understanding the Weather	Creating a graph	Writing a prediction		Making predictions
30. Understanding Tables: Working as a Wildlife Specialist	Using tables	Writing an analysis		Making predictions
31. Figuring Pay: Should You Be Your Own Boss?	Making calculations	Writing an analysis		Analyzing information
32. Using Formulas: Explaining Measurements	Using formulas	Writing an explanation		
33. Explaining Financial Data: Writing a Speech	Understanding financial charts	Writing an informative speech		
34. Explaining Statistics: Writing an Ad	Statistics	Writing an ad		
35. Understanding Charts: Tracking Your Nutrition	Understanding charts; percentages	Writing an analysis		Analyzing information
36. Analyzing a Budget: How You Spend Money	Budgeting	Writing an analysis		Analyzing information

Cooperative Learning

The math writing projects in *Writing in Mathematics* can often be adapted for group learning. In study after study, educators have discovered that when students learn together, there are powerful benefits. Perhaps the most important gain is in classroom cohesion. When students feel they are part of a group, they often feel good about themselves and their performance improves. They also have been found to work harder, to sacrifice more for each other, and to feel happier in the classroom.

There are suggestions for incorporating cooperative learning within activities on pages 8–17. Here are some tips for making cooperative learning a success.

Choose the groups with care. If individuals are not getting along, give them a chance to develop an understanding of one another by placing them together and asking them to work together. Avoid self-selected groups that isolate less-popular class members.

Make the group size appropriate to the project. Because it is important for everyone in the group to have a role in the project, make sure there is enough work for everyone in the group.

Ensure that everyone in the group has an essential role. There should be a way for every person in the group to become involved—in fact, it should be necessary to enlist everyone's help to get the project done.

Have group members divide tasks and create a time line for completion. Have students decide on what tasks need to be done, when they need to be done, and who is responsible. Then have a group member write the agreement so that there are no misunderstandings later on. As the project proceeds, build in a periodic progress review.

Place the responsibility with the students. This is their project. Make sure everyone knows the consequences of not performing his or her part, and then let students reap the rewards for their success.

Create an event worth waiting for. If students are successful, they deserve to see their efforts rewarded. This can mean presenting their work to another class or having the video, book, or other project they created available in the library for others to check out.

ESL/LEP Strategies

Non-English or limited-English speakers face several challenges. They must learn the mechanics of the language, but they also must learn to interpret the cultural signals and messages that native and long-time speakers of the language send one another. They also risk being labeled by other students or their teachers as slow learners because they do not understand English.

Here are some guidelines for helping non-English speakers and limited English speakers benefit from *Writing in Mathematics*.

1. Have another student read the instructions aloud. When students hear language, they can more easily grasp the meanings of words through emphasis and intonation.

2. Have students make a list of unfamiliar words and expressions that can later be defined by you or another student.

3. Help students define unfamiliar words and idioms. Idioms, in particular, can be perplexing for language learners.

4. If possible, pair a proficient English speaker with a less proficient one. Both students can gain a deeper understanding of language by analyzing it in detail.

5. Emphasize activities that feature visual and oral ways for students to gain information.

6. Explain the task in several ways—repetition, paraphrasing, restatement, use of synonyms—so students have several chances to understand what is being asked of them.

7. Have students explain what they just read. This technique is useful in judging whether a student understands directions and whether he or she understands a passage.

8. Model what you want. Give an example of what a completed lesson might look like. You might also want to use visual examples if you can.

9. In some cultures, students who do not understand directions or concepts are not encouraged to speak up. Make sure that ESL/LEP students in your classroom know that they are encouraged to ask for explanations.

10. Create opportunities for ESL and LEP students to choose subjects or use examples from their native countries.

11. Encourage students to write, even though they will make errors. Emphasize the general content over the mechanics, especially at first.

12. Have a proficient English speaker help an ESL/LEP student revise his or her writing.

Assessment

Evaluating student writing can become an opportunity rather than a chore. It can provide you with a clear record of student progress as well as telling you where students need help.

There are several ways to judge the quality of student writing. One way is to have students assess themselves. (See the reproducible masters for student self-evaluation forms.) What grade would they give this effort? Where do they think they need improvement? In some cases, students may need your help for this exercise. They may know that something doesn't sound or feel right but be unable to pinpoint why. Students can use their first assessment as a way toward writing another version of their work to be judged by you.

Peer evaluation can also be a successful method of assessment. Students work in small groups, with each student taking turns reading his or her work and receiving comments from peers about the effectiveness of the writing and where it could use improvement. Encourage students to be objective and constructive when they assess one another's work. You might also model the evaluation procedure by making a first comment in which you point out one or two strengths of a student's work and then pinpoint an area that needs clarification or additional development. Modeling respect for student work can often set a tone that students can easily follow.

As you look at student work with an eye to assessing it, look at first drafts as works in progress. Your nonjudgmental comments can provide a chance for students to see the possibility for improvement in their work. In a rough draft, first look at and respond to the ideas; execution comes second. By the time the student has turned in his or her final draft, assessment can occur on a number of levels, ranging from ideas to mechanics.

Keeping those factors in mind, student work can be judged on a scale of 1 to 5. A *1* indicates the work is not adequate and needs considerable revision. A *3* indicates that work is acceptable but could be improved, and a *5* indicates that the work is outstanding, with little or no revision needed.

Here is a checklist of things to look for when assessing student writing. Not all these criteria may apply to every lesson in this book.

	1 (WEAK)	3 (AVERAGE)	5 (EXCELLENT)
Topic	too broad or narrow; unfocused	adequate choice of topic	well-defined, interesting topic
Purpose and audience	unclear purpose; inappropriate material for audience	purpose is adequately stated; material is appropriate for audience	purpose is clearly stated; material engages audience
Organization	poor or no organization of material	average organization; some problem with the flow of ideas	material is well organized, flows clearly from one point to the next
Main idea and details	hard to tell main ideas; details irrelevant or nonexistent	fair amount of detail; Some main ideas not stated clearly or supported	main idea stated clearly; details are precise and support main points
Vocabulary	words used incorrectly	not enough variety in word usage	words carefully chosen to achieve writer's purpose
Spelling	many incorrectly spelled words	several incorrectly spelled words	all words correct
Grammar	mistake use of parts of speech; run-on sentences; sentence fragments; problems with subject-verb agreement	some problems with parts of speech, subject-verb agreement	few to no mistakes in grammar
Punctuation	misused or no punctuation	some mistakes in punctuation	few to no mistakes in punctuation

Teaching Strategies

DEVELOPING MATH SKILLS

Lesson 1

Taking Notes: Reading

Teaching Notes: You might want to model good note-taking technique with a section of a textbook.

Cooperative Learning: To have students evaluate their note-taking abilities, have them take notes independently, and then compare notes to see how different students wrote them. Finally, have each group write a set of notes that incorporates the best of the individual efforts. Groups can then compare their notes.

ESL/LEP Strategies: Suggest that ESL/LEP students make a separate list of words they do not understand. Students might want to keep such a list in a separate notebook. Have them leave several spaces after each word or phrase so that later they can write in a definition for the word.

Lesson 2

Lesson 2. Taking Notes: Listening

Teaching Notes: This is a good model lesson to do with a lesson you teach. If necessary students can take turns using their notes to reteach the class.

Extension Activities: There are several shows on public television stations that focus on math. Have students watch one, take notes, and report to the class on what they learned.

Cooperative Learning: Have students listen as a group and then divide up into smaller groups to compare their notes. They can see who took the best notes and why and construct a set of master notes for the class.

ESL/LEP Strategies: Tell students to watch for gestures and inflections that impart meaning. For example, show them the body language you use when explaining something particularly important.

Lesson 3

Lesson 3. Math Methods: Guess and Test

Teaching Notes: Model the Guess and Test process in the classroom. If students don't seem to understand it, go through the process again, asking different students to help you with different parts of the process and different examples.

Extension Activities: Students might want to practice using this technique with other disciplines.

ESL/LEP Strategies: Many people learning a new language still think in their first language. Because this is primarily an exercise in thinking out loud, some ESL/LEP students may find this exercise frustrating. If students are having trouble using this method, have them do it bilingually: They can first think and write in their native language and then translate the process into English. Once students feel they are proficient at using the method, have them try to do it first in English.

Lesson 4

Math Methods: Problem Solving

Teaching Notes: The point of this lesson is to free up students from using a rote approach to learning math. You can model how to approach a problem from different ways and ask students how they do alternative problem solving in their everyday life.

For example, give students this problem: They need to find a way home from school, they have no money, and it's too far to walk. How do they get home? Have students brainstorm ideas, and explain that brainstorming can be useful in solving math problems, too.

Cooperative Learning: Because much of this technique depends on having a creative approach to solving problems, it is a good one for cooperative learning. Students can put their heads together and brainstorm alternative ways of solving problems. You might want to divide the class into groups, give the class a problem to solve, and see which group can come up with the most ways to solve it.

ESL/LEP Strategies: Invite students to use diagrams to help them do their alternate approaches to solving a math problem and to try to put their diagrams into words after they have finished.

Lesson 5
Math Methods: Working Backward

Teaching Notes: This is another way to help students look at math problems. Explain that it is actually the way they look at many problems in their lives. Give the example of an allowance and a wish list: The student would have to work backward from the amount of allowance money available and then decide how to spend it. Ask students for other examples of this technique in everyday life.

Extension Activities: For a week, have students record the number of times they work backward to solve a problem. At the end of the week, make a list on the board with everyone's examples.

Lesson 6
Math Methods: Using Mental Math

Teaching Notes: This lesson has instant applicability to students' lives. Point that out as you introduce the lesson: In a day, a student might well use this method at a store to see if he or she could afford something, while measuring something, such as fabric, or when trying to decide how much paint to buy. This lesson is also an example of thinking out loud to reach an answer. You could have student volunteers answer mental math problems posed by other students in a round-robin exercise. Have students tell their thinking as they solve the problems.

Extension Activities: Students can keep track of the times they use mental math in a week, writing the problems and how they solved them.

ESL/LEP Strategies: If students do not understand the instructions on how to do mental math, pair them with English speakers who can work with them to explain the process.

Lesson 7
Explaining Math: Writing a Lesson

Teaching Notes: This can be one of the most successful ways to bolster weak students and give exceptional students a chance to learn. You might want to assign student-led lessons as a matter of routine; every Friday, for example, you could choose a different student to teach a review class of the week's work. Easier concepts could be taught by weaker students to help them gain confidence; more difficult classes could be reviewed by excellent students. You could also pair a high achiever with a low achiever to work on a lesson plan together.

Extension Activities: Use student lessons to create an alternative math book. Have students help you design the book and choose the lessons to be included.

Cooperative Learning: Try this approach to teach reviewing for a big test: Divide the class into groups so that the students who are having trouble with a concept will be teaching it.

ESL/LEP Strategies: Pair an ESL/LEP student with one proficient in English. Have them work to create a bilingual lesson—with the caveat that both students have to do at least some teaching in the other language.

Lesson 8 — Explaining Math: Writing a Real-Life Test

Teaching Notes: Show students good examples of word problems and analyze with them why these problems work. After students have analyzed the problems, have them help you make a list of tips for constructing these tests.

Extension Activities: Make a book of students' questions that students can use to review for tests. Keep an answer key (checked for accuracy) in the back of the book.

ESL/LEP Strategies: Invite students to create problems that showcase their cultural heritage.

REAL-LIFE MATH

Lesson 9 — Everyday Math: Keeping a Math Journal

Teaching Notes: If you are studying a specific topic that students are likely to see or use in their environments, direct students to that topic.

Extension Activities: Begin a bulletin-board display of math at work. Invite students to illustrate the math they have seen at work around them, and add it to the bulletin board.

ESL/LEP Strategies: Suggest that students write about different kinds of everyday math they saw in their native homes. For example, students may find that shopkeepers deal with money differently in their native countries than they do here. Have students make notes about those differences in their journals. Encourage students who are having trouble explaining mathematical principles in English to make notes in their native language and then translate them later with the help of a friend.

Lesson 10 — Analyzing Information: Creating a Bar Graph

Teaching Notes: There are bar graphs in the financial section (and other sections) of the newspaper daily. Bring them in as examples to show students how bar graphs are used. You might want to collect enough so that students can take turns explaining them. Discuss with students why people use bar graphs to illustrate information; point out that it is often easier to understand and compare information when it is in a bar graph. To illustrate your point, have students compare the information that is presented in words on the first page of the lesson with the bar graphs they created. Which is easier to understand?

Extension Activities: Have students make humorous bar graphs about aspects of their lives. For example, they could graph how many times their brother slams a door during the days of a week or the number of times they listen to the same song on the radio during different hours. Have students post their bar graphs in the classroom.

Lesson 11 — Gathering Data: A Public-Attitude Survey

Teaching Notes: Public-attitude surveys are becoming increasingly common. Have students cut opinion surveys out of the newspaper for a week or so before you do this lesson. Then discuss the surveys the class collected. How were they done? How many people were asked? Were the questions fair?

Extension Activities: If students' surveys unearth interesting data, be prepared to take their research farther. Who would be interested in knowing the results of this survey? How could your students publicize what they have learned?

Cooperative Learning: Because the process of asking a large sample of people can be time consuming, this is an ideal project for a cooperative learning project. Review the tips for cooperative learning on page 4.

Lesson 12 — Using Math: Writing a Persuasive Letter

Teaching Notes: Ask students about persuasive writing they have read. Ask them to give examples. Which examples most impressed them? Why? You might want to cut out some persuasive letters to the editor and read them to the class. Which work best? Why?

Extension Activities: Have students take the results of the previous lesson and write a persuasive letter based on the information they gathered. You might want to post student efforts on the board or have students mail their letters to people who might be influenced by their results.

ESL/LEP Strategies: Use the letters you brought in to point out how the writers used the language to help make their points.

Lesson 13 — Lesson 13. Using Fractions: Computing a Recipe

Teaching Notes: Model this lesson with a recipe you bring from home. You might want to make enough for the class to illustrate the importance of getting the fractions right.

Extension Activities: There are several ways to use this lesson. One is as a culminating lesson for a unit on fractions. Another is for a class picnic or a team-teaching lesson with a teacher doing a geography or family history unit, where students make the food. You could also create a book of recipes intended for large groups. Have the class write an introduction about the art (and math) of increasing quantity in recipes.

Cooperative Learning: This can be a good cooperative learning lesson if the lesson is continued with a party in which the recipes are used. Divide students into groups so that each has both a recipe to do for the party and another task, such as invitations, buying supplies, or cleaning up. Have the groups each check the math in each others' recipes.

Lesson 14 — Estimating: The Costs of Running a Car

Teaching Notes: Estimating is a skill that students probably use more often than they think. Make a list on the board of ways in which students estimate daily. You could prompt them with these questions: Do you estimate how much money you'll need during a day? Do you estimate how long it will take to walk somewhere? Do you estimate the amount of food you need to cook dinner for your family?

Extension Activities: Students can choose something else to estimate if their family doesn't have a car or if they are uninterested in the subject. Have them approve their choice with you.

ESL/LEP Strategies: If students are having trouble understanding the directions, have them highlight words and concepts they do not understand and make guesses in the margins. Check the guesses, and help students make new ones if their first guesses are inaccurate.

WRITING MATH REPORTS

Lesson 15. Writing a Short Paper: Explaining Math History

Lesson 15

Teaching Notes: Writing this paper can provide a good introduction to the idea of explaining the history of math ideas. When students have proven that they can handle a short paper, you might want to have them research and write a report as outlined in Lessons 16–20.

Extension Activities: Encourage students to present their papers using art. They can use illustrations, photographs, charts, graphs, or whatever visual aids they think will be most effective to reinforce the paper's points and capture readers' attention. If the reports are impressive, consider displaying them in the classroom or creating a book with them.

ESL/LEP Strategies: Pair ESL/LEP students with English-proficient students to help them work on their papers. Encourage students to find subjects that relate to their native countries or their heritage.

Writing a Report: Choosing a Topic

Lesson 16

Teaching Notes: Model the process of selecting and limiting a topic. Have the class give you a suggestion for a broad topic. Then, using students' suggestions, think out loud about how you could refine a topic, rejecting topics that are too broad and too narrow and selecting one that is interesting and able to be done.

Extension Activities: Find examples of good report writing about math topics. Ask students to find other examples. Collect the examples, and display them in a folder that students can look to for reference.

Writing a Report: Taking Notes

Lesson 17

Teaching Notes: Have students review Lesson 1, on taking notes, on page 2 of the student book. You might also want to review the concept of plagiarism with the class. Write the word on the board, and have students discuss what it means. Many resources in libraries today are computerized. Before doing this lesson, you may want to have your librarian review how to retrieve information using a computer. You may also see if your librarian will give a general lesson on using library resources to locate information.

Extension Activities: Take your class on a field trip to your local library, where the librarian can explain how to find information.

ESL/LEP Strategies: Consider sending your ESL/LEP students to the library with a student who is an experienced researcher and can give students a familiarization tour of the library.

Writing a Report: Creating an Outline

Lesson 18

Teaching Notes: To give students more experience working with outlines, have them outline an article or paper. Then have students trade articles and papers and critique each other's work. As students begin work on their own outlines, point out that this part of writing a report is often the most frustrating. There are likely to be stray facts that don't fit in any pile, other facts and information that could fit in more than one place, and confusion about what should constitute a separate group of cards. If you sense that your students are becoming frustrated, model the process for them by using one student's notes with the class. Also remind students that they can continue to revise their outlines until they are satisfied.

Cooperative Learning: Another way for students to gain practice outlining is to put them in small groups to outline each student's paper in turn.

Lesson 19 — Writing a Report: The First Draft

Teaching Notes: After students have finished their first drafts, have them underline and label the parts: the introduction, the thesis sentence, the main points and supporting details, and the conclusion.

Cooperative Learning: You may want to use a peer review process to help students improve their first drafts. Divide students into small groups. Have them all place their papers, without names, in a folder and then hold a writer's critique about each paper, listing first the strengths and then the weaknesses of each report.

ESL/LEP Strategies: First drafts should tell you whether students understand the principles of writing a report. You may want to tell ESL/LEP students that they can write a shorter paper, as long as they show you they understand what they are doing.

Writing a Report: Revising and Footnotes

Lesson 20

Teaching Notes: Make sure students use the checklist in the lesson before revising their papers. To reinforce the importance of using the checklist, you might want to go over each of the points in detail, asking students to explain each.

Extension Activities: Have students create resource lists for class use. In this list, have students write their bibliographic information, plus a short description of what the book or resource contains, and how much the student liked it. You can keep these resource lists in the classroom, filed by subject, for students to add to throughout the year.

THINKING OF MATH IN WORDS

Lesson 21 — Math Fun: Writing a Logic Game

Teaching Notes: Students enjoy these logic games. Once they have written their games, they can trade them and play them.

Extension Strategies: Have the class create a book of their games, and put it in the library for other students to check out.

ESL/LEP Strategies: Have students create bilingual versions of their games.

Lesson 22 — Describing Math: What's a Million?

Teaching Notes: Write one million and one billion in numerals on the board to give students a feeling for the numbers. Talk about ways that these numbers might be represented. *The Guinness Book of World Records* contains many examples of the use of these figures.

Extension Activities: Some schools have collected a million pennies and then used the money for specific projects or for charity. This lesson might make a good starting point for a field trip to understand the amount of money a large bank handles during a day. If students come up with good descriptions, create a bulletin-board display in the hall for the school to see.

Lesson 23

Explaining Math: Writing a Book for Children

Teaching Notes: Check some books from the library that explain math to third graders, and let the students look at them ahead of time. When you are ready to do the lesson, gather the books and show them again to the students. Discuss which ones work best, which are the most clear, and which ones children might find the most appealing.

Extension Activities: Publish the books. Give them to a third-grade teacher to use and have the third graders look at the books and grade them.

Cooperative Learning: You may want to have students work in groups to conceptualize, write, illustrate, and publish their books.

ESL/LEP Strategies: There is a real need for bilingual books to explain concepts such as those in math. Encourage students to write bilingual books, explaining that in this case, the fewer words, the better, as long as the concepts are clear.

MATH AT WORK

Lesson 24

Lesson 24. Estimating : Writing a Carpenter's Bid

Teaching Notes: Discuss with students a building project they have been involved with at home. What steps did they go through to design the project and to decide costs?

Extension Activities: Bring in copies of ads from the Sunday newspaper placed by home improvement stores. Have students create their own projects and decide how much each would cost using the prices in the ads. Students can call for the prices of materials that are not advertised.

Cooperative Learning: Do the extension activity as a cooperative learning project. Have each group do a presentation to the class as if they were giving a bid to a prospective client.

ESL/LEP Strategies: Students may be unfamiliar with some of the words and phrases concerned with carpentry. Have them highlight unfamiliar words so that you or another student can explain them.

Lesson 25

Planning Costs: Working as a Travel Agent

Teaching Notes: Review Lesson 5, Working Backward, on page 10 of the student book with students. Model the steps of working backward on a similar project; for example, show them how you might work backward with a budget to do a dinner party, and explain the similarity of the project to this lesson. To interest students in this lesson, bring in some travel brochures from different locations to show students.

Extension Activities: Have students take the results from this lesson and use it to create a window display for a travel agency, a package vacation brochure, or a letter to clients explaining the dream vacations they can buy for $4,000. You could also have a travel agent come to class and explain how he or she uses math in planning trips.

Cooperative Learning: Have groups work on this project, following the cooperative learning guidelines on page 4.

ESL/LEP Strategies: Some of the shorthand language of the travel industry may be unfamiliar to these students. Explain terms such as cruise, airfare, and hotel package.

Lesson 26 — Estimating Costs and Profits: Planning a Service Business

Teaching Notes: Brainstorm with students the kinds of businesses they might want to run or have some experience running. Next, brainstorm the answers to the questions they will be answering.

Cooperative Learning: Students can work in groups on this project. If students come up with a project that might work and they seem enthusiastic about pursuing it, encourage them to see if the project could become reality.

Lesson 27 — Figuring Discount: Writing an Ad for Your Business

Teaching Notes: It is not necessary for students to have done the previous lesson for them to do this one. You can have them write an ad for an already existing business. You might want to bring in examples of ads in which discounts are used to lure customers and discuss whether students pay attention to such information when they read ads.

Extension Activities: Use the student ads as more practice for figuring discounts. Have students trade their ads with other students, attaching a shopping list. Have students figure how much the items on the shopping list would cost. Have the ad writer check the work.

ESL/LEP Strategies: These students may not understand some of the terms used in the ads you bring in. Explain unfamiliar terminology.

Lesson 28 — Using Statistics: Working as a Baseball Writer

Teaching Notes: Begin the class with a discussion of sports and its obsession with statistics. What importance do they have for teams? for players? for players' salaries? How can statistics be deceptive?

Extension Activities: If you have students in your class who are fascinated by sports, have them do a similar exercise with other kinds of sports statistics. You might even have these students plan presentations for the class in which they explain the meanings of the statistics for a specific sport.

Cooperative Learning: Students who are interested in this topic could form a group to do a talk-show presentation for the rest of the students. Have four or five students each pose as experts on the statistics of different sports. Then you could have the students plan a talk show with the topic: "Sports Statistics: What Do They Mean?"

ESL/LEP Strategies: Students may be fans of sports popular in their countries but not as popular here. Have them prepare a talk for the class explaining the sport and how statistics play a part in that sport.

Lesson 29 — Lesson 29. Making Predictions: Understanding the Weather

Teaching Notes: Emphasize the importance of weather forecasts by making a list on the board of people for whom being able to predict the weather is crucial. If students are having trouble with this question, write gardeners, rafting company owners, and clothing store owners on the board and have students discuss why the weather is important to these people.

Extension Activities: Have students make their own record of the high and low temperatures for the month and figure the average, high, and median temperatures.

ESL/LEP Strategies: Have students listen to a few weathercasts and keep notes of words or phrases they do not understand. They can add them to their vocabulary list and have you or another student define them.

Lesson 30   Understanding Tables: Working as a Wildlife Specialist

Teaching Notes: Discuss with students how charts and graphs often have to be read in conjunction with one another to make sense of them.

Extension Activities: Have students research an animal on the endangered-species list and make a table that explains what has happened to the animal since it was declared an endangered species.

APPLYING MATH

Lesson 31   Figuring Pay: Should You Be Your Own Boss?

Teaching Notes: This lesson is a good example of how math becomes useful in everyday life. Tell students that this situation is one that some people face and that making the right decision could have a big impact on their lives. Make a list of other ways that students use math now or think they may use it in the future.

Extension Activities: Have students read the employment ads in the classified section of the newspaper on Sunday. Then have them choose a job that they think they might be interested in and figure out the benefits and pay they would receive from three similar jobs advertised in the paper.

ESL/LEP Strategies: Explain some of the conventions of the tax and payroll system to students who are unfamiliar with them.

Lesson 32   Using Formulas: Explaining Measurements

Teaching Notes: Ask if anyone has ever been in another country. Ask the person to describe his or her experiences, trying to translate everyday measurements, such as money and temperature. If no one has been to another country, describe an imaginary journey to another country and the ways in which the students would need math to be able to cope. Point out that without some math skills, the trip would be less enjoyable.

Extension Activities: Students can write other sections of the book having to do with translating: For example, have students explain how to convert currency for different countries (using exchange rates from a local bank).

ESL/LEP Strategies: Students can explain the different kinds of measurements and conversions that would be necessary if students were to visit their native country.

Lesson 33   Explaining Financial Data: Writing a Speech

Teaching Notes: Bring in the financial pages of the newspaper. Then ask students who are interested in this information how the economic trends in the country impact their lives—examples could include loan rates, inflation, and savings interest.

Extension Activities: Consider having a banker come into the class after students have finished this activity. The banker could give his or her explanations of the financial charts in the paper and why they are important to everyone.

ESL/LEP Strategies: Make sure you define unfamiliar words for these students.

Lesson 34 — Explaining Statistics: Writing an Ad

Teaching Notes: If your state has a lottery, bring in some ads. Ask students to think about them. Why are they written the way they are? What do the writers of the ads hope to accomplish?

Extension Activities: If your state has legalized gambling, compare the odds on winning at various games. Ask students why they think gambling is illegal in many states.

Cooperative Learning: Have a group construct an entire ad campaign using the information they develop from this lesson. The ad campaign can include a slogan, ads for magazines and newspapers, radio and TV ads, and a mailer that could be sent to people throughout the state.

Lesson 35 — Understanding Charts: Tracking Your Nutrition

Teaching Notes: Bring some books to school that contain nutritional values of foods to help students with this activity. Remind them that the nutrition figures on food are based on a serving size that may not match what they are eating. Make sure they adjust their nutrition figures to reflect how much they are eating. After students have completed this activity, ask them to discuss what they discovered. Were they surprised? What, if anything, do they plan to change to help make them healthier?

Extension Activities: Have a nutritionist visit the classroom to explain the genesis of the nutrition chart on the back of prepared foods. You could also have the nutritionist explain the different components the label analyzes.

Cooperative Learning: Have students divide into groups and use this chart to analyze the lunches at school for a week. Then have them work to create an analysis of the week. You might want to see if you could get the information published in your school newspaper.

Lesson 36 — Analyzing a Budget: How You Spend Money

Teaching Notes: Their own money is a subject of great interest to students—just as it is to all of us. Discuss with your class the problems students have keeping to a budget, how they plan to buy things they can't afford now, and some of the consequences of impulse buying. Ask if any students have budget advice for the others—approaches that have worked, tricks to keep track of their money.

Extension Activities: Have students keep track of their budgets as part of their weekly homework. At the end of two months, have students report on their progress at keeping track of where their money goes and planning for future financial needs.

Answer Key

Developing Math Skills 1. Notes should reflect the main points and supporting evidence of the reading material. **2.** The speaker's key points and the details that support those points should be clear in the notes. **3.** Assess answers for clarity—answers should clearly describe students' thinking. **4.** Look at answers for evidence that students can use alternate methods for problem solving. **5.** Answers should show how students thought through the problem. **6.** Sentences should describe how students reached the answers by using these techniques. **7.** Assess student lessons for organization, clarity, and coherence. **8.** Make sure that students' word questions test the concepts in the lesson and that they show the ability to apply knowledge from the lesson.

Real-Life Math 9. Watch for student entries that apply everyday experiences to the use of math. **10.** Answers should show that football food is most expensive, baseball and hockey higher on some items, lower on others. **11.** Criteria for questions: free of bias, narrow, easily understood. **12.** Letter should contain facts and evidence to support opinion. **13.** Correct proportions should be shown; recipes should have directions adjusted for quantity. **14.** Answer should contain clear explanation of costs.

Writing Math Reports 15. Report should be interesting, well organized, and support key points with details. **16.** Check topic for interest and narrow focus. **17.** Students should use correct style in quoting authors and taking notes. **18.** Outline should show good organization. **19.** Students may want to refer to General Writing Tips on page 75 of the student book. First draft should include introduction, body, and conclusion. **20.** Have students use self-assessment reproducible master in this Teacher's Manual. Revision should have few mechanical errors and flow organizationally.

Thinking of Math in Words 21. Answer to logic game: left house: The Joneses, photography; middle house: The Ramons, hiking; right house: The Barneses, camping. **22.** Look for descriptions that offer a striking and correct comparison. **23.** Book should explain topic clearly and correctly.

Math at Work 24. Correct totals: $102.24 (plywood); $40.78 (counter); $600 (labor); $97.16 (overhead); Job total: $906.88. **25.** Answers should be supported by cost and value comparisons. **26.** Watch for correct assumptions and realistic analysis. **27.** Ad's discounts should be realistic and accurate. **28.** 1.) Pct. is number of games converted into percentage figure. 2.) GB is games behind the leader. If Colo wins one game and first place team doesn't play, the two teams are tied for first. 3.) 119 times; he hit the ball to reach base a little fewer than 4 times for each 10 times at bat. 4.) Seitzer; he hits better. 5.) American League. **29.** Trends: High 50s, 60s in early part of month, 60s and 70s later. **30.** Memo should indicate that snoutfish population rose when program focused on increasing gillfish population. To continue this trend, the program should continue to support the gillfish population.

Applying Math 31. $1,487.50 self-employed; $1,540 as employee. Financially, student would be better off as employee. **32.** Explanations should be clear and understandable. **33.** Data shows: unemployment down; loan rate down; stock prices up—economic trends are good. **34.** Ad should emphasize slim odds of winning, and fact that only half goes to prizes. **35.** Have students double-check figures. **36.** Answers should show recognition of ways to improve financial management.

Writing Self-Assessment

Name _____ **Date** _____ **Lesson** _____

Use this sheet to help you evaluate your writing. A *5* is the highest rating; a *1* is the lowest.

Areas	Rating	Comments and Examples
Content		
Content soundness. Is the content thoughtful and accurate?		
Interest. Is the paper interesting?		
Appropriateness. Is the content right for the audience and purpose?		
Topic. Is the topic narrow enough?		
Main idea. Is there a clear main idea and thesis statement?		
Details. Is there supporting evidence and details to support main ideas?		
Introduction. Does it catch the reader's attention? Does it tell the main point of your paper?		
Conclusion. Does it contain a restatement of the main idea?		
Title. Does the title reflect the subject of the paper? Is it interesting?		
Organization		
Order. Is the content arranged logically and effectively?		
Unity. Do all the ideas and details in the paper support your key point?		
Connections. Do the points flow smoothly from one to the other?		
Usage, Mechanics, Style		
Clarity. Is the writing clear? Do the sentences make sense?		
Sentence Style. Are the sentences varied in length and structure?		
Correctness. Is the paper free of punctuation, grammar, and spelling errors?		

Writing Mechanics Checklist

Name _____ **Date** _____ **Lesson** _____

After you write, check your work against this list.

Paragraphs

☐ Did I construct paragraphs correctly? Look for:

Topic sentence

Paragraphs that contain sentences with details that support the topic sentence within the paragraph

Sentence Structure

☐ Were all my sentences complete? Look for:

Run-on sentences that should be split into two sentences

Sentence fragments that do not have a subject and a verb

Word Usage

☐ Did I use words correctly? Look for:

Agreement of subjects and verbs (incorrect: "I weren't ready.")

Correct use of adjectives and adverbs (incorrect: "doing good")

Correct form of pronouns (incorrect: "Me and him went home.")

Punctuation

☐ Did I use punctuation correctly? Look for correct use of:

Commas (incorrect: "Then he did, not do it.")

Periods (incorrect: "St James Street")

Semicolons (incorrect: "She said; come here.")

Colons (incorrect: "I wasn't ready: and he wasn't either.")

Parentheses (incorrect: "The word means (blue).")

Quotation marks (incorrect: "So go, I said, "and he did.")

Capitalization

☐ Did I capitalize words correctly? Did I capitalize:

First words of sentences (incorrect: "he went")

Initials (incorrect: "s. j. Peters")

Proper nouns (incorrect: "baltimore")

Titles (incorrect: "dr. Brown")

Spelling

☐ Did I watch for:

Correct spelling of plurals (incorrect: "geeses")

Correct spelling of possessive forms (incorrect: "it's tail is wagging")

The Writing Process: Brainstorming

Name _____ **Date** _____

When you brainstorm, you explore ideas without thinking if they are right or wrong, or if they fit or don't fit. You just let you mind wander. Use this page to help you brainstorm a topic to write about. Write down whatever comes to mind.

1. What topics are you interested in? _____

_____

_____

2. Pick one of the topics you wrote that interests you the most. Write it here: _____

_____

_____

3. Look at the topic you wrote. Write other ideas that come to mind when you think about this topic.

_____

_____

_____

_____

4. Write another topic that interests you. Write it here. _____

_____

_____

5. Look at the topic you wrote. Write other ideas that come to mind when you think about this topic.

_____

_____

_____

_____

6. Look at all the ideas you wrote. Highlight or circle the ones that interest you the most.

The Writing Process: Organizing Ideas

Name _____ **Date** _____

Use this graphic aid to organize your thoughts as you plan your paper. You might want to write the statement that describes your report in the center circle, with a main point in each outer circle and supporting facts underneath.

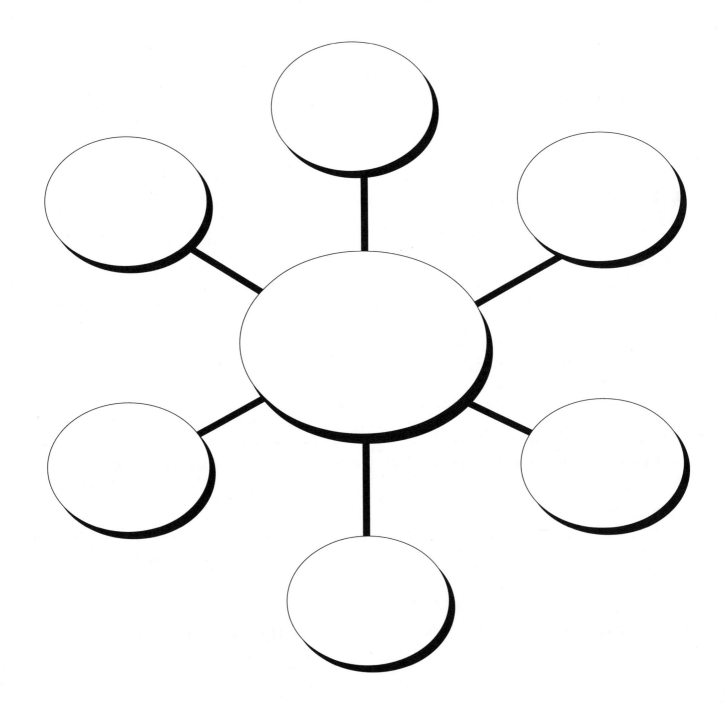

The Writing Process: Checking Your Outline

Name _____ **Date** _____

Sometimes, taking another look at your outline after you write can be helpful. It can show you whether you made all the points you wanted to make. It can show you if you did not follow your outline when you wrote your paper. Sometimes, that means your outline could have been better. Sometimes, it means that your paper should be revised to match your outline more closely.

Look at your paper. Write an outline of what you wrote here.

_____

_____

_____

_____

_____

_____

_____

_____

_____

_____

_____

_____

_____

_____

_____

The Writing Process: Drafting a Paragraph

Name _____ **Date** _____

Use this space to write a first draft of a paragraph. Do not worry about spelling or punctuation now. You can correct any errors later. As you write, refer to the guidelines on the left side of the page. Use them along with your notes to help you organize your draft. You may want to use this organizer to help you write other paragraphs in your report.

Include a topic sentence that gives the main idea of your paragraph.

_____
_____
_____
_____

Write your first fact. Write the details that support your first fact.

_____
_____
_____
_____
_____

Write your second fact. Write the details that support your second fact.

_____
_____
_____
_____

Continue writing facts and details that support them until you have written all the facts that support your topic sentence.

_____
_____
_____
_____
_____

Write a concluding sentence that restates your main idea.

_____
_____

The Writing Process: Revising

Name _____ **Date** _____

TALK IT OVER

Work with a partner. Listen as your partner reads his or her paragraph aloud. During the first reading, listen for the main point your partner is making and for the facts presented to support the main point. After the first reading, try to answer these questions.

1. What is the main point of the paragraph? Where is it stated?

2. Is the topic sentence in the most effective place? If not, where else could it be placed?

3. Do the facts support the main point? Which do and which don't?

4. Does the writing flow smoothly from one point to the next?

Switch roles. Have your partner follow the same steps with your paragraph.

MAKE THE CHANGES

Reread the paragraph. Do you need to add facts or to make smoother transitions? Think about your partner's comments and suggestions. Make any changes that will improve your paragraph. Copy the revised paragraph on a clean sheet of paper.

PROOFREADING

This is the final revision before turning in your work. These are the proofreading marks that editors use to correct errors.

∧ add something	⸝⸜ add quotation marks
⸜ delete something	⁋ new paragraph
≡ capitalize (b)	/ lower case (B̸)
⊙ add a period	(SP) spell correctly
⸝∧ add a comma	∪ transpose (s∪i means "is", for example)

Reread your paragraph and correct errors in spelling and punctuation using proofreader's marks. Switch work with your partner, and read each other's work for errors.

FINAL COPY

Write a final, clean copy of your work, with all the errors corrected.

Creating a Bar Graph

Name _____ **Date** _____

Graphs organize information and show how it is related. A bar graph shows information as a series of horizontal bars or vertical columns. Use this page to help you construct a bar graph.

1. What data do you want to display? _____

_____

2. What should the title of your graph be? _____

_____

3. What information do you want on the bottom line (the horizontal axis)? _____

_____

4. What information do you want on the vertical line (the vertical axis)? _____

_____

Remember that you need to divide each axis into sections. For example, if you are creating a bar graph about what happened in different years, each year would be a different section.

Use this space to create your bar graph.

Title: _____

Information on
vertical axis

_____

Information on
horizonal axis:

_____

Creating a Circle Graph

Name _____ **Date** _____

When you make a circle graph, you divide a circle into wedges that approximate each number. Use this page to help you make your circle graph.

1. Convert the data to decimals. Divide each number by the total number.

2. Calculate the angle of each section by multiplying the decimal value of each category by 360 (the number of degrees in a circle).

3. Draw each wedge using a protractor. Label the pie chart.

Writing Word Problems

Name _____ **Date** _____

Use this worksheet to help you create word problems based on the work you are doing. Write the problem in the left column. The test taker uses the right column to make calculations. Keep the answers on another sheet.

1. _____

_____

_____

_____

_____

_____ **Answer**

2. _____ _____

_____

_____

_____

_____

_____ **Answer**

3. _____ _____

_____

_____

_____

_____ **Answer**

_____

Creating a Flow Chart to Run a Business

Name _____ **Date** _____

Fill in this flow chart to help you make decisions.

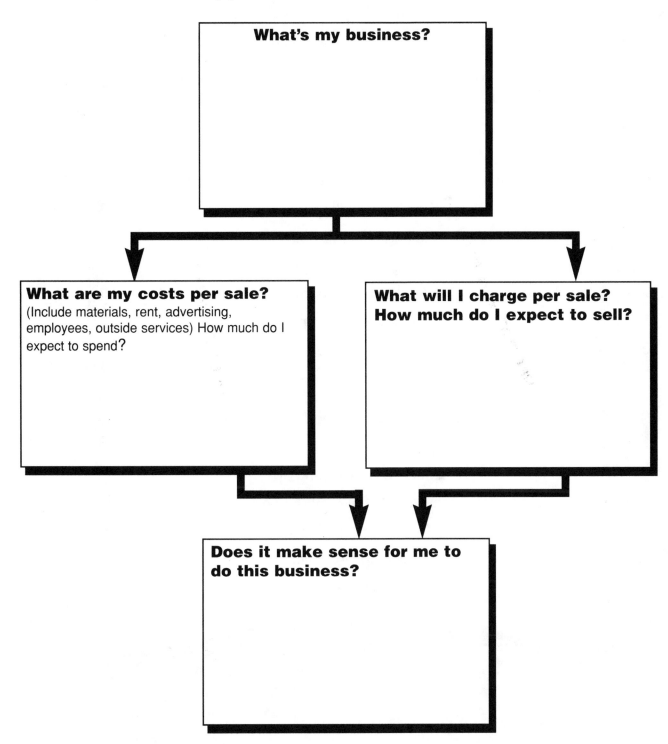

What's my business?

What are my costs per sale?
(Include materials, rent, advertising, employees, outside services) How much do I expect to spend?

What will I charge per sale? How much do I expect to sell?

Does it make sense for me to do this business?

WRITING ACROSS THE CURRICULUM

WRITING IN
MATHEMATICS

This worktext will help your students become more successful writers in your mathematics classes. In the student's book, you will find models for writing, tips and diagrams for organizing ideas, and guidelines for getting started.

Among the 36 student lessons, you will find:

Keeping a math journal

Taking effective notes

Using math strategies

Analyzing math data

Writing a math report

Analyzing a budget

Explaining math history

See these features in the *Teacher's Resource Manual*:

Reproducible activity sheets

Cooperative learning tips

Activities for ESL/LEP students

Assessment guidelines

Teaching strategies

Answer keys

GLOBE FEARON EDUCATIONAL PUBLISHER
A Division of Simon & Schuster
Upper Saddle River, New Jersey

ISBN 0-8359-1896-3

90000

9 780835 918961

What You'll WRITE

1. Use this space to explain to your investors—people who loan you money for expenses like this ad and who expect to be paid back—what you will be offering in your ad. Explain the amount you will lose by the discounts you will be offering and how you expect to make up for these losses with extra guaranteed income. _____

_____

_____

_____

_____

_____

_____

2. Use this page to design your ad. Sketch the art you want to include. Make sure that you mention:

❑ what your service is

❑ why people should use your service rather than someone else's

❑ how much people will save using the discounts you are offering

28 Using Statistics
LESSON
Working as a Baseball Writer

What You'll LEARN

The business of sports is often one of statistics. A baseball player's worth to his team can be decided by his stats. In this activity, you'll explain baseball statistics.

What You'll DO

You're a sportswriter answering questions in the "Ask the Sportswriter" column for your newspaper. Look at these charts for standings in the major leagues, and think about how you'll answer the fans' questions.

MAJOR-LEAGUE TEAM STANDINGS

N.L. WEST

	W	L	Pct.	GB	Lst10	Streak	Home	Away
San Fran.	23	17	.575	–	8-2	Won 2	14-8	9-9
Colorado	22	17	.564	1/2	7-3	Won 2	14-6	8-11
Los Angeles	20	20	.500	3	7-3	Won 5	8-11	12-9
San Diego	17	22	.436	51/2	5-5	Lost 1	13-11	4-11

N.L. CENTRAL

	W	L	Pct.	GB	Lst10	Streak	Home	Away
Cincinnati	24	14	.632	–	7-3	Lost 1	12-8	12-6
Chicago	22	16	.579	2	4-6	Lost 3	7-7	15-9
Houston	19	18	.514	41/2	6-4	Lost 2	7-11	12-7
St. Louis	16	25	.390	91/2	4-6	Lost 2	9-12	7-13
Pittsburgh	14	23	.378	91/2	2-8	Won 1	5-11	9-12

N.L. EAST

	W	L	Pct.	GB	Lst10	Streak	Home	Away
Phila.	25	14	.641	–	4-6	Won 1	12-6	13-8
Atlanta	22	17	.564	3	5-5	Won 3	12-11	10-6
Montreal	22	19	.537	4	4-6	Lost 4	13-7	9-12
New York	15	24	.385	10	4-6	Lost 2	8-11	7-13
Florida	11	26	.297	13	4-6	Won 2	4-14	7-12

NATIONAL LEAGUE
BATTING (Through Tuesday)

Based on 3.1 plate appearances for each game player's team has played.

	G	AB	R	H	AVG
Barile, NY	36	134	27	51	.381
Williams, SF	38	137	27	49	.358
Offerman, LA	36	132	29	47	.356
Larkin, Cin	37	149	25	53	.356
Biohette, Col	37	130	24	50	.350
R. Sanders, Cin	36	139	24	44	.338
Bonilla, NY	36	139	23	47	.338
Gwynn, SD	38	148	23	50	.338

PITCHING
ERA

Perez, MIL	1.76
Maddux, ATL	2.20
B. Jones, NY	2.33
Valdes, LA	2.39
Martinez, Mtl	2.53
Fasscro, Mtl	2.63
Navarro, Chi	2.84
Wilson, SF	2.68
Leiter, SF	2.74
Barile, NY	2.78

AMERICAN LEAGUE
BATTING (Through Tuesday)

Based on 3.1 plate appearances for each game player's team has played.

	G	AB	R	H	AVG
Seltzer, Mil	32	119	11	46	.387
Davis, Cal	38	138	30	52	.377
Naehring, Bos	36	129	23	47	.364
Ramirez, Bos	36	128	28	46	.359
Ramirez, Clev	37	135	30	48	.356
E. Martinez, Sea	31	140	24	48	.343
Gibson, Det	36	139	25	33	.327
Baerga, Clev	38	154	25	50	.325

What You'll WRITE Use the major-league team standings on page 56 to answer these questions from your column's readers. Remember that you are writing for a newspaper audience.

1. What does the *Pct.* (percent) column mean? Explain what Pittsburgh's Pct. of .378 means. _____

_____

_____

_____

2. Explain the *GB* (Games Behind) column. What does the 1/2 in that column mean to Colorado?_____

_____

_____

_____

3. I don't understand how baseball figures batting averages. For instance, how often did the leader, Milwaukee's Seitzer, hit the ball? Explain what his .387 average means.

_____

_____

_____

_____

4. Look at the statistics for the American League players Baerga and Seitzer. Based on their AB (at bat) numbers, their hits, and their runs, which player would you prefer to have on your team? Why?_____

_____

_____

_____

_____

5. Contrast the batting averages for the National and American Leagues. Which league do you think has better hitters? Explain. _____

_____

_____

_____

Making Predictions
Understanding the Weather
LESSON 29

What You'll LEARN

Weathercasters use math to look at the past and predict the future. In this exercise, you'll learn how they do it.

What You'll DO

You're the substitute weathercaster for tonight's broadcast. Because it is May 1, you are checking information about weather in the first half of May from previous years. You will predict what is likely to happen based on the past. Here are the tables you were given.

HIGH TEMPERATURES, Degrees Fahrenheit, 1920–1995

May	1920	1930	1940	1950	1960	1970	1980	1990	1993	1994	1995
1	59	57	69	55	77	57	58	69	70	68	65
2	57	55	67	64	70	55	60	54	66	58	69
3	59	56	66	56	70	67	68	58	68	60	68
4	57	60	68	58	72	79	70	59	69	70	68
5	58	62	63	58	73	69	69	64	66	69	70
6	54	60	67	56	73	70	66	59	68	78	77
7	60	62	63	67	65	77	68	67	66	70	72
8	62	70	67	70	71	70	70	72	69	69	73
9	64	64	67	68	65	73	72	70	80	69	75
10	59	68	66	69	60	72	72	69	71	70	70
11	58	68	67	68	69	71	71	73	77	69	70
12	60	60	59	70	72	77	73	73	77	70	71
13	60	60	64	64	66	70	70	72	73	77	77
14	61	66	62	63	70	71	77	73	77	75	74
15	66	64	63	66	68	69	70	70	76	73	64

WEATHER CONDITIONS, 1920–1995

Day	1920	1930	1940	1950	1960	1970	1980	1990	1993	1994	1995
1	sun	cloud	cloud	sun	rain	sun	cloud	cloud	cloud	rain	sun
2	cloud	cloud	cloud	rain	rain	rain	rain	cloud	sun	rain	rain
3	cloud	rain	cloud	rain	sun	cloud	cloud	cloud	sun	rain	sun
4	cloud	cloud	sun	rain	cloud	cloud	rain	sun	sun	rain	cloud
5	sun	cloud	rain	rain	rain	cloud	sun	rain	rain	rain	cloud
6	sun	cloud	cloud	cloud	rain	cloud	cloud	rain	rain	sun	sun
7	sun	sun	sun	rain	cloud	cloud	cloud	sun	rain	rain	rain
8	sun	sun	rain	rain	cloud	cloud	cloud	rain	rain	rain	sun
9	cloud	sun	sun	sun	cloud	rain	sun	cloud	cloud	rain	sun
10	cloud	sun	sun	sun	sun	sun	cloud	cloud	cloud	cloud	sun
11	sun	sun	sun	sun	cloud	cloud	sun	sun	cloud	cloud	sun
12	sun	sun	sun	sun	cloud	cloud	sun	sun	sun	sun	sun
13	cloud	sun	sun	cloud	sun	sun	sun	sun	sun	sun	sun
14	cloud	sun	sun	sun	sun	sun	sun	sun	sun	sun	sun
15	rain	sun	sun	sun	sun	cloud	cloud	sun	cloud	sun	sun

What You'll WRITE

Your job is to interpret the data in the tables above. You must tell your viewers what they should expect during the first half of May. Figure the average high temperature for each day, and report what the trend is during the first part of the month.

On another piece of paper, create a graph that shows your viewers what the weather conditions are likely to be in the first half of May, based on the past. If you need help creating the graph, see Lesson 10, Analyzing Information: Creating a Bar Graph, on page 20.

You may want to include in your weathercast any interesting facts you gather from the tables. Remember to write as if you were talking to a friend. Use short sentences that are easy for listeners to follow. Write your weathercast on another piece of paper.

30 Understanding Tables
LESSON

Working as a Wildlife Specialist

What You'll LEARN

People who work with endangered species keep records about how species are doing so they can see if their efforts are successful. In this activity, you'll interpret these tables and write a memo to your boss.

What You'll DO

You have just been given this chart about the numbers of living snoutfish, an endangered species that has been tagged so that its numbers can be measured. The chart also contains information about the numbers of living gillfish. Snoutfish eat gillfish. Look at the numbers and predict what will happen to the population of snoutfish.

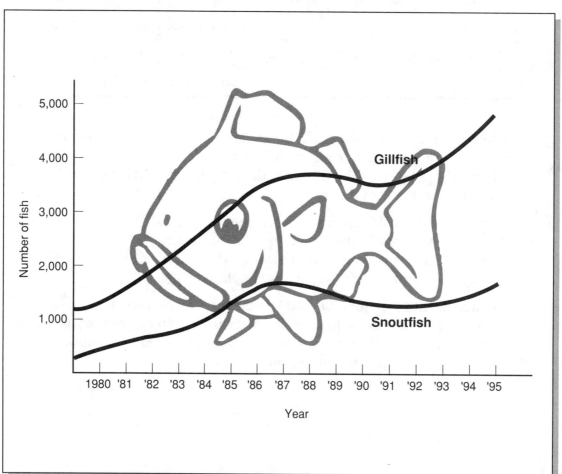

Your boss wants a report about the success of the snoutfish program. The program began in 1980. Since then, the snoutfish program has included these measures:

From 1980 to 1985, the program tried to increase the number of gillfish.
From 1983 to 1990, the program focused on cleaning the water.
From 1990 to 1995, the program worked on increasing the number of gillfish again.

Write a memo to your boss explaining how successful the different parts of the program have been. Make recommendations about what should be done next. Also, use the chart to help you predict the future numbers of snoutfish if current conditions continue.

Use the following form for your memo:

MEMO

TO: Supervisor

FROM: _____

RE: Snoutfish program

_____

_____

_____

_____

_____

_____

_____

_____

_____

_____

_____

_____

_____

_____

_____

_____

_____

31 Figuring Pay
LESSON
Should You Be Your Own Boss?

What You'll LEARN
You have the choice of becoming a full-time employee of a company or becoming an independent contractor. An independent contractor works for himself or herself. In this activity, you'll learn how to decide which position makes more economic sense.

What You'll DO
Here are the figures that explain how much you would earn if you were your own boss and how much you would earn if you accepted the job offer and became an employee. Analyze the information.

Independent Contractor	Employee
earns $2,350 per month	earns $1,700 per month
health insurance: $240 per month	health insurance: $80 month
self-employment tax: 15% of salary	no self-employment tax
materials cost: $150 month	materials supplied: no cost
daycare: $120 weekly	daycare: $80 weekly

What You'll WRITE   Write a letter to the company telling the president if you are accepting the job offer. In your letter, analyze the benefits of both possibilities. Then explain why you made your decision. If you need tips for writing a business letter, look back at Lesson 24, Estimating: Writing a Carpenter's Bid, on page 48.

_____
_____
_____
_____
_____
_____
_____
_____
_____
_____
_____
_____
_____
_____
_____
_____
_____
_____
_____
_____
_____
_____
_____
_____
_____

32 Using Formulas
Explaining Measurements

LESSON 32

What You'll LEARN

Being able to convert temperature from Celsius to Fahrenheit and the U.S. system of yards and feet to metric measurements can be important when you're using or buying products made in another country. In this activity, you'll get some practice making the change.

What You'll DO

You work for a company that publishes travel guides. As part of a new series for U.S. travelers, the editor wants a section on how to convert U.S. measurements to those more often used in foreign companies.

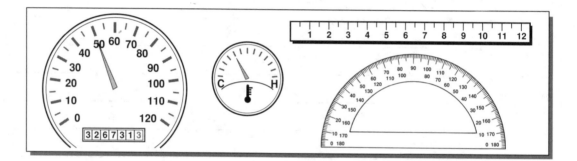

Here is some information about the systems and formulas to convert them:

- If C = degrees Celsius and F = degrees Fahrenheit, the conversion formula from Fahrenheit to Celsius is $C = 5/9(F-32)$.

- To convert Fahrenheit approximately to Celsius, subtract 30 from the Fahrenheit reading and divide the answer in half.

- To convert Celsius to Fahrenheit, the formula is $F = 1.8 \times C + 32$.

- To convert Celsius approximately to Fahrenheit, $2 \times C + 30 = F$.

- If m = meters and $in.$ = inches, the conversion formula for meters to inches is $m \times 39.37 = in.$ To change inches into feet, divide by 12.

- To convert inches into centimeters (cm), $in. \times 2.54 = cm$.

- If mi = miles and k = kilometers, to convert miles to kilometers, $mi \times 1.6 = k$.

- To convert miles approximately to kilometers, $mi \times 3$ divided by $2 = k$.

- To convert kilometers to miles, $k \times 625 = mi$.

- To convert kilometers approximately to miles, $k \times 2/3 = mi$.

What You'll WRITE Write the conversion section of the travel guides that allow U.S. citizens to change U.S. measurements to metric measurements and Fahrenheit temperatures to Celsius temperatures. Remember to make your writing easy to understand so that anyone picking up the book could make these conversions. Include examples.

_____

_____

_____

_____

_____

_____

_____

_____

_____

_____

_____

_____

_____

_____

_____

_____

_____

_____

_____

_____

_____

_____

_____

33 Explaining Financial Data
LESSON **Writing a Speech**

What You'll LEARN

The daily newspaper contains graphs and charts of how the national economy is doing. You can learn to analyze these figures and decide for yourself what is happening with the economy.

What You'll Do

Read these graphs and charts.

WORLD INDEX In U.S. dollars

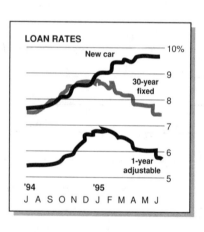

LOAN RATES

New car

30-year fixed

1-year adjustable

'94 '95
J A S O N D J F M A M J

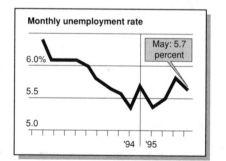

Monthly unemployment rate

May: 5.7 percent

6.0%

5.5

5.0

'94 '95

- Looking at this graph, you can tell that the world stock markets have been on a fairly steady course during the two years shown.

- The phrases "30-year fixed" and "1-year adjustable" refer to rates for loans on houses. During April of 1995, for example, a 1-year adjustable rate for a home loan was about 6 percent.

- Looking at the line that refers to the monthly unemployment rate, you can see that the rate has gone down from its high above 6% in early 1994.

- You can tell from looking at this chart that throughout 1995, the value of stocks in the Standard and Poor's Index has risen steadily.

What You'll WRITE You will analyze the charts on page 66 and write a short speech for your Economics Club about what the charts mean for the economy of the United States. Tell the club members where these measures have been going in the past few months and where it looks like they might be headed.

_____

_____

_____

_____

_____

_____

_____

_____

_____

_____

_____

_____

_____

_____

_____

_____

_____

_____

_____

_____

_____

_____

_____

_____

_____

_____

_____

34 Explaining Statistics
Writing an Ad

LESSON

What You'll LEARN

Does it make sense to bet in a state lottery? What are the chances of winning the jackpot? Find out in this activity.

What You'll DO

You're in charge of writing the ads to persuade voters to vote against a proposed state lottery. The lottery would allow people to buy a ticket for $1 and choose six numbers from 1 to 42. The lottery then chooses six numbers. This chart explains a person's chances of winning prize money, depending on how many winning numbers he or she chose.

Number of Winning Numbers	Probability of Winning
3 of 61	in 37
4 of 61	in 556
5 of 61	in 24,287
6 of 6	1 in 5,245,786

In the lottery, about 50 percent of the money collected goes to prizes. The rest goes to lottery administration and state revenue.

People win very little if they only match three of six numbers; those who match all six win at least $1 million.

The "6 of 6" jackpot winner can choose to have his or her prize money given out over 25 years, which means 1/25th of the prize would be given each year. The jackpot winner can also choose to take the money in a lump sum. If he or she does that, he or she gets only 40 percent of the advertised jackpot.

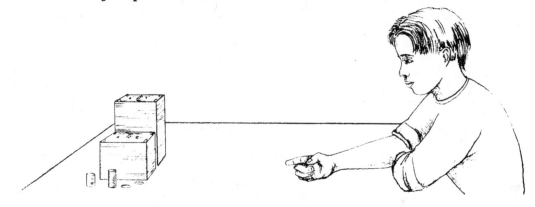

What You'll WRITE Answer in complete sentences these questions about the lottery. Then write the copy, or words, for an ad designed to convince people that they should vote against the lottery.

1. What are the chances that a person who buys one ticket for a dollar will win the jackpot?

_____

_____

_____

2. Compare the chances of a person's winning the jackpot in the lottery with his or her chances to achieving some other goal. _____

_____

_____

_____

3. Write your advertisement in the space below. Remember to write it in a way that gets people's attention and that anyone can understand. You may also use drawings to make your point.

35 Understanding Charts
LESSON
Tracking Your Nutrition

What You'll LEARN You can learn to analyze what you eat and see how you can make your diet more healthful.

What You'll DO Make a list on which you write everything you eat during one day. If you eat prepared food, check the nutrition information on the package. If you eat fresh food, estimate the amount you eat.

What You'll WRITE Keep track of the amount of fat and carbohydrates (simple and complex) you eat in one day.

1. Fill in this chart to track your fat and carbohydrates for a day.

Food	Grams of Fat	Grams of Complex Carbohydrates	Grams of Simple Carbohydrates (sugar)

2. Write an analysis of your fat and carbohydrate intake. In your analysis, include the percentage of fat in your diet. Also include how many complex carbohydrates and how many simple carbohydrates (sugars) you ate in one day. Then write how you could improve your diet.

_____

_____

_____

_____

_____

_____

_____

_____

_____

_____

_____

_____

_____

_____

36 Analyzing a Budget

LESSON

How You Spend Money

What You'll LEARN

You can analyze how you are spending your money and plan how to use it to reach your goals.

What You'll DO

What do you think you spend your money on? What do you really spend it on? You'll find out in this activity.

First, write what you think your budget is for a month. Write your budget in two columns. One should be income (allowance, baby-sitting fees, lawn-mowing jobs, gifts for your birthday, etc.). The other column should include what you think you spend your money on. This could include anything from snacks to clothes to savings.

Here is one student's estimated monthly budget:

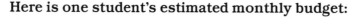

Income		Expenses	
fast-food job:	$435	taxes:	$ 79
interest from savings:	$ 15	clothing:	$130
		college savings:	$ 55
		entertainment:	$75

When she finished her budget, this student was surprised to realize that although she had $450 monthly in income, she could account for only $339. She kept better records the next month. She found out that she was spending more on clothes than she thought and that she was also spending $60 monthly on food. She looked at her budget and decided to change her spending so that she could save more for college.

What You'll WRITE

Like this student, you can see what you are really earning and spending. You can also decide how to change your spending habits to reach your goals.

1. Write your estimated budget income and expenses here:

Income: _____

_____

_____

_____

_____

Expenses: _____

_____

_____

_____

_____

_____

_____

_____

2. For the next month, keep records of your actual expenses and income.

Income: _____

_____

_____

_____

_____

Expenses: _____

_____

_____

_____

_____

_____

_____

3. Use the information you gathered in the first two questions to create pie charts for your actual and budgeted income and expenses. To create a pie chart, follow these steps:

a. Convert your data to decimals. Divide the amount of dollars spent (or earned) for each item by the total number of dollars in your budget.

b. Calculate the size of each section of the pie chart. Multiply the decimal value of each category by 360 (the number of degrees in a circle).

c. Fill in the pie charts below, dividing and labeling them with the approximate amount you budget and the amount you spend during one month. Estimate each category.

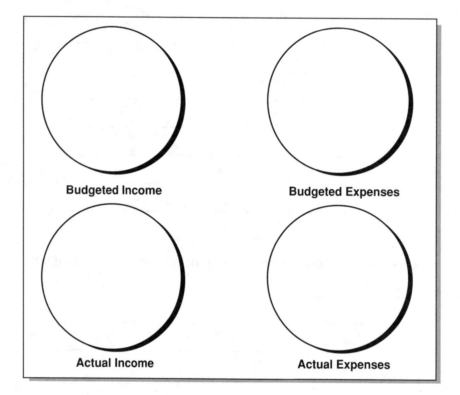

Budgeted Income   **Budgeted Expenses**

Actual Income   **Actual Expenses**

4. Write how you plan to change your spending and income to reach your goals.

_____

_____

_____

_____

_____

_____

_____

Writing Checklist

You may write a letter to apply for a job or a letter to a friend about a baseball game. No matter what you're writing, you can use this checklist to help you make sure that your ideas are heard and understood.

Prewriting. Before you pick up a pencil, you need to do some thinking about what you'll write and how you'll write. Answer these questions as you plan your writing:

❏ What is my purpose? Why am I writing? What message do I want to communicate?

❏ Who is my audience? Who will read my work? Answering this question will help you decide how you will write. If you are writing a letter to apply for a job, your letter will probably be formal. If it is a letter to a friend, your letter will have a friendlier tone.

❏ What kind of writing will I be doing? There are many different types of writing. These include letters, speeches, notes, and reports. You need to decide which kind of writing you'll be doing.

Research and Organizing. You need to know what you're writing about. In research papers, you may be doing formal research. In letters to persuade, you may need to gather facts. In this stage, you need to find information about your subject.

❏ Should I write an outline? For most types of writing, it makes sense to outline or even make a brief list of your main points. When you write your first draft, you can turn your outline into paragraphs.

Drafting. This is where you write the information you've gathered. In this stage, don't worry about grammar or punctuation. Put your ideas down, keeping these questions in mind:

❏ Do I have an introduction that tells the reader what I plan to say?

❏ Do I make my main points and use details to support them?

❏ Does my writing flow from one point to the next?

❏ Does my conclusion briefly restate the main point of the writing?

Revising. Here are questions to think about as you look over and revise your first draft:

❏ Have I checked my spelling, grammar, and punctuation?

❏ Have I read my writing to see if I can use better words or cut out unnecessary ones?

❏ Is my writing interesting? Would other people want to read it?

Preparing a Final Copy. After you have revised your writing, share it with a friend. Ask him or her the questions in the drafting and revising sections. Use the responses as a guide to creating your final draft. Then write or type a clean copy of your work.

WRITING IN
MATHEMATICS

WELD COUNTY SCHOOL DISTRICT RE-3 CO

GLOBE FEARON EDUCATIONAL PUBLISHER
A Division of Simon & Schuster
Upper Saddle River, New Jersey

Executive Editor: Barbara Levadi

Project Editors: Lynn W. Kloss, Laura Baselice, and Bernice Golden

Writer: Sandra Widener

Production Manager: Penny Gibson

Production Editor: Nicole Cypher

Marketing Managers: Sandra Hutchison and Nancy Surridge

Interior Electronic Design: Richard Puder Design

Illustrators: Accurate Art and Andre V. Malok

Electronic Page Production: Paradigm Design

Cover Design: Mimi Raihl

Printed in the United States of America.
6 7 8 9 10 03 02 01 00
BF2

ISBN: 0835-91895-5

GLOBE FEARON EDUCATIONAL PUBLISHER
A Division of Simon & Schuster
Upper Saddle River, New Jersey

Contents